Proud parents

Gay men and lesbians share
their experiences of adopting
and long-term fostering

Nicola Hill

Published by
British Association for Adoption & Fostering
(BAAF)
Saffron House
6-10 Kirby Street
London EC1N 8TS
www.baaf.org.uk

Charity registration 275689 (England and Wales);
SC039337 (Scotland)

British Library Cataloguing in Publication Data
A catalogue record for this book is available from the British Library

ISBN 978 1 907585 66 1

Project management by Shaila Shah, BAAF
Cover design by Helen Joubert Designs
Cover photo courtesy of www.istockphoto.com
Designed and typeset by Fravashi Aga
Printed in Great Britain by TJ International

Trade distribution by Turnaround Publisher Services, Unit 3, Olympia Trading Estate,
Coburg Road, London N22 6TZ

BAAF is the leading UK-wide membership organisation for all those concerned with
adoption, fostering and child care issues.

Contents

ACKNOWLEDGEMENTS

I would like to thank all the contributors to this book who generously gave their time and shared their experiences; Shaila Shah for suggesting the idea for the book; Andy Leary-May, Director of New Family Social, and Phil Reay-Smith for helping me to find contributors; Laura McCaffrey for reading and commenting on the first draft of the book; and Isabel Atherton, my agent, for handling my contract. Thanks also to Jennie Lazenby for her advice. She is one of the people who oversaw the book, *Lesbian and Gay Fostering and Adoption: Extraordinary Yet Ordinary*, published in 1998.

NOTE ABOUT THE AUTHOR

Nicola Hill is a writer, specialising in LGBT issues. Previous publications include *A Very Pink Wedding*, a book about civil partnerships, published by HarperCollins and *The Pink Guide to Adoption*, published by BAAF. She also offers training and gives presentations about recruiting adopters and foster carers from the LGBT community.

Nicola and her partner, Laura, foster two children on a long-term basis.

Foreword

David Akinsanya

Broadcaster David Akinsanya grew up in the
care system and now fosters and mentors children
in care. From his early days in the Who Cares?
Movement, David has always campaigned for
looked after children.

Sadly, I was never given the chance to be adopted or fostered on a long-
term basis. A combination of my father's desire to keep me in his life and
the fact that adoption was not as prominent as it is today meant I spent all
of my childhood in a children's home.

In the 1960s and 70s, adoption was not as transparent – a lot of children
discovered they were adopted in later life and many dual heritage kids
were confused about having white parents. We have moved on a lot
since then.

The closure of many children's homes and the "part privatisation" of the
care system mean that adoption and long-term fostering have become
a big issue.

The recent drive to rely more on adoption as an option for children
unable to live with their parents has put a lot of pressure on children's
services. Whether this is being done as a way of saving money (adoption
is the cheapest option compared to fostering or residential care) or

because it is genuinely better for children is an important debate.

Another important change is that we no longer deny that children have a birth family and letterbox and/or face-to-face contact is usually part of the deal.

As well as attitudes towards adoption changing, attitudes towards lesbian and gay adopters and foster carers are changing for the better. The work of Brighton and Hove and other forward-thinking local authorities to encourage and support lesbian and gay people to adopt and foster is an important step forward.

When I made the Channel 4 series, *Find me a Family*, the biggest reaction to the programme was to John and Anthony, the gay couple featured. I was so happy that we had lots of people contacting us about them. Thankfully, it was all positive. The scene where they had to care for a disabled child touched so many people – some saying that they hadn't agreed with gay men adopting but seeing this couple in action had totally changed their minds.

Perhaps society, with all its prejudices, has overlooked lesbian and gay adopters and foster carers for too long. Adoption and long-term fostering can be many things to many people. From those who can't have children to people who want to do something to help – adoption and long-term fostering can be the answer.

For some lesbian and gay people, the desire to nurture is great and not having a child can leave a large hole in our lives. There is a growing and desperate need for more people to adopt and foster. I think it is high time local authorities and agencies fully embraced the lesbian and gay community as it is still a largely untapped resource. Being lesbian or gay should no longer mean that we can be overlooked. The system needs us.

This book should be read by lesbians and gay men – to encourage more to come forward as adopters or foster carers. It should also be read by social workers to show them how we can provide supportive, loving families for children who need our care.

Introduction

In compiling this book, I have been very moved by people's stories, and struck by their patience, resilience and determination to give children a better chance in life. All of them have adopted children or fostered them on a long-term basis.

I have interviewed a wide range of people – from a single, lesbian carer fostering teenage boys to gay men who adopted a baby girl. Some have already had children of their own, others wanted to create a new family or make a difference in their local community.

All of them have made enormous changes in their lives, often giving up a carefree existence, exotic holidays, city trips, clubbing and lie-ins! Many have said that as much as they enjoyed this lifestyle, and sometimes miss aspects of it, they knew they wanted to do something else with their lives.

That "something else" can often start by responding to an advert in a newspaper or magazine or attending an open evening run by a local authority or voluntary adoption agency. Taking that first step is enormously brave and may be the culmination of years of talking about fostering and/or adoption but never quite doing anything about it.

The people featured in this book talk about their motivation to take that first step and their experience of going through the assessment process, allowing social workers to probe into their lives. They have all survived the experience – some even enjoying it – and gone on to have children placed with them. One couple, who initially fostered and then adopted, had two children turn up on the doorstep with a social worker in the middle of the night as an emergency, but most have met the children through planned introductions, taking place over several weeks.

There are some vivid descriptions of those first stages of a new life together, including one child who was so excited to have his own clothes for the first time that he spent an hour trying them on, even though the house was strewn with new toys.

Others have dealt with the children's understandably strong reactions to being moved – breaking toys in anger, urinating on carpets or soiling themselves. Some have experienced difficulties in the children attaching to them and vice versa. One woman describes a breakthrough moment when she finally bonded with her adopted daughter.

From these early stages, the contributors to this book have shared how they have established boundaries, rewards and sanctions, tried out new activities, taken children on holidays for the first time and introduced them to their families and friends. They have also advocated for the children to ensure they get the best out of children's social services, education and health authorities – no mean feat.

Gay men and lesbians also talk of proud moments when their children first learn to read, win awards, or cook a meal. They discuss the impact of adoption and/or fostering on their own lives, relationships, finances and work. Some are also at the stage of preparing their children for independence. They tell their stories with honesty and give sound advice.

I asked people about being lesbian or gay parents and whether this made any difference to their parenting or their children's experiences. Some felt there was a positive impact, while others were so busy parenting, they thought their sexuality was insignificant. I also interviewed some of the children about their experiences of being brought up by lesbians or gay men. They were all positive about their experiences and one 14-year-old boy said he didn't think gay men or lesbians should be afraid to become foster carers or adopters.

I challenge anyone who has ever thought that lesbians and gay men should not be parents to read this book and not be moved. With an increasing number of children coming into the care system, more lesbians and gay men should be encouraged by society to come forward and take the first step towards becoming adopters or foster carers. I hope this book helps to prove that we can make a difference to young people's lives.

All names of contributors and their children have been changed to protect their identity.

1   Eduardo and Colin

> Eduardo, 45, who is dual heritage, works for a large blue-chip company and his partner, Colin, 48, white British, is a craftsman. They adopted two children, Josephine, when she was 14 months old and Finlay, aged 11 months. The children are now aged eight and five respectively. Eduardo and Colin have recently been assessed for a third child. They live together in the south of England.
>
> Eduardo tells their story.

What prompted you to adopt?

I come from a large, Catholic family with 21 cousins. My mother is white British and my father is Mediterranean. All my brothers and sisters have children. I never thought it was possible to have children as a gay man and I wish we had thought of adoption earlier. As it was, I had to adopt as a single person and Colin got a care order. This was before the law changed allowing gay couples to adopt. I would have adopted more children if we had started younger.

Nine years ago, we responded to an advertisement in the local newspaper. We were assessed by the local authority. We hadn't expressed a preference for either sex and had assumed we would get a boy. Soon after we had been approved, Social Services rang us out of the blue and said they thought they had a match. I said, 'What's his name?' I was very surprised to find out they were considering a girl. We were approved in the January and Josephine moved in at Easter.

Josephine's mother was a very young mum. She was living in a mother and baby unit but wanted to relinquish her baby. It was very traumatic when we met Josephine's mum – she was delightful but very young. I think given the right circumstances, she could have made it work.

When we applied to adopt the second time around, there was a 14-month gap between approval and placement. Finlay was the youngest of 15 siblings who had all been taken into care. He was placed in emergency foster care when his mother was unable to cope and was neglecting him. He had two foster care placements before being adopted.

What have you learned about yourself?

I think it's been the making of me. I used to be much more self-centred before I had children. Now you have to put them first, but it's worth it for the joy they give you. It's hard work but very satisfying and gratifying. Both the kids are very loving and giving.

I have learned to be patient and very forgiving. I used to be intolerant. I've also learned to pace myself. I would get up at six in the morning to get everything done. I used to be bleaching everything, as we have cats and dogs. I can't do that now with two children. You have to take things more in your stride. I remember being much more anxious the first time around.

Have you had any disappointments?

Not really, but I would say we are not pushy parents. We just want them to be happy. I think if your expectations are too high, you set yourself up for disappointment.

And any surprises?

Some essential information about our second child wasn't disclosed prior to the placement. He is actually deaf in one ear. We felt a bit aggrieved about that, especially considering we had met the paediatrician on the matching panel. We were prepared to take a child with a disability, but adoption is about choice and we weren't given any choice. But obviously, there is no going back now.

We have heard about this happening quite a lot, with social workers witholding information about children, a bit like a crafty car dealer. If they were more honest, placements might work out better.

What has worked well for you?

I think preparation is the key to everything. As two men, we hadn't had much hands-on experience so we worked in a nursery once a week as part of our preparation. We also did a positive parenting course, some training at BAAF and a residential course. That really worked well for us. I've also read loads on attachment disorder. We did lots of nesting, getting their rooms ready.

When each child moved in, we tried to keep the same routines as the foster homes for the first few months. The change is so massive for them. If you can keep some things the same, it is less traumatic. As neither of ours could speak when they were placed, we had to guess quite a lot. I would say find out as much as you can from those who have cared for them beforehand.

What has been your experience of the adoption agencies?

We should have had more clarity and transparency from the social workers. You should be able to read the entire file on the children.

We adopted through our local authority the first time and found a match with a local authority quite far from where we live the second time. There has been a lack of consistency and consensus between the two different authorities that we have dealt with. We wouldn't go out of area again. If I did my job to the same standard as the local authorities, my company would close down. We were sent someone else's home study (the confidential report made on prospective adopters), we saw a copy of an email sent from a manager to our social worker, saying: 'My money's on the gays, let the others down gently', when they were considering us and other couples.

I believe the so-called matching process is a big fallacy. It is pot luck but it shouldn't be. It is people's lives we are dealing with. Apart from sex and age, there is no matching, it is just a question of who is available, and if a social worker isn't fighting your corner, forget it.

Both of us are really dark-skinned and yet the two children placed with us are very blond – I've had people ask if their mother is Scandinavian. It's ridiculous, from day one, we said we were happy to have a child that didn't match our ethnic background, but that was seen as a complete no-no. We saw a child advertised in a magazine and rang up to enquire, as he looked like me. However, they said he was one-eighth African-Caribbean and we were told we would not be considered for a child with a different ethnic background. He was still being advertised in the magazine three months later.

I feel we have had to jump through more hoops as a gay male couple. We had to prove that we could change a nappy and had my sister and her child stay for a month. Other dads on the course didn't have to offer as much evidence of childcare. They also asked if our relationship was deep and meaningful. We've been together 20 years. Some of the adopting heterosexual couples had only been together a few years.

They also asked questions such as, 'How are you going to cope at the school gates or talking to other mums?' – I'm sure they didn't ask other dads the same questions.

What difference do you think you have made to the children's lives?
I feel we have enriched their lives, offering them continuity and consistency. They have two dads who love them and put them first. We also have a very fortunate lifestyle. We travel a lot and have a home overseas. If they had stayed where they were, they wouldn't have had the same opportunities and would have had a different lifestyle.

What impact has adoption had on your lives?

You don't visualise how much it is going to change your life. When Josephine came along we were in a complete daze for three months. Children need constant attention. You can try to keep life fresh but it is governed by the children, their routines, bottle-feeding, sleeps, etc. Both of ours slept for two to three hours in the afternoon, which was good, but you can't do much around the house because you don't want to make any noise.

Most of our friends BC (before children) were people without kids, so some of them trailed off. You can't socialise nearly as much and you need to be in bed by 11pm, but on the other hand, there comes a stage in life when you don't want to be the oldest clubber in town.

You don't realise how much holidays are going to cost with children as prices are so much higher in the school holidays.

I wouldn't change it for the world but I would caution young gay men or those who haven't been together for very long against having a baby or a young child. However, there are 28 lesbian and gay families in our area and half are male and they have stuck at it.

And on your finances?

We are managing at the moment but as the children get older it will cost more. We are fortunate as we both have semi-decent jobs but I have gone part-time. When we adopted eight years ago, I only received six months' pay at the statutory maternity rate, which is peanuts. I actually stayed at home for the first 18 months in order to bond with our first child. You want to do your best for the children and the importance of attachment is drummed into you. They have already suffered separation and loss, so if you can stay at home, it is best, especially at the beginning. We didn't even put our daughter in a nursery for the first year and even in the second year, it was only for two hours, two to three days a week. I don't think it is good to abdicate responsibility and put them in day care.

With the second child, the battle to get "maternity leave" was much easier. I was something of a test case but I secured nine months' full pay and six months at the maternity rate, followed by three months' unpaid leave. They also kept in touch and sent me on an eight-day back-to-work course. I was the only bloke on the course with 19 women.

What impact has adoption had on your relationship?

It does make you less available for the other person. You have to follow routines, so it is harder to be spontaneous. You have to work out your difficulties before considering adoption. If you are on wobbly territory, don't think adoption will fix it – the cracks in your relationship will come under enormous pressure and it is not fair on the children.

The children have to come first and you can get jealous of the amount of time they take up. Sexually speaking, you have to fit it in after they have gone to bed and often you are tired by then. You also can't be as liberal about nudity.

How do you share parenting responsibility?

We are really good at presenting a united front. It is not good if you have different parenting styles – the children get confused. If there is anything you disagree with, you have to handle it when the kids have gone to bed, not in front of them. If you are not consistent, they will pick up on it and press buttons. Luckily, Colin and I are from the same school of parenting, we are fussy about table manners and tidying rooms, washing hands and saying please and thank you.

We all sit down and eat together at the table. We teach them that sharing is caring. We do a lot of refereeing but you have to challenge bad behaviour because if it goes unchecked it can become an issue. The children seem to have feelings of injustice and can easily feel that you are picking on them. Sometimes they can be co-operative and other times "Mr Angry" comes to the surface and you don't know why. They are challenging but you have to be strong, have clear boundaries, give clear instructions and check that they understand you.

How have you discussed your sexuality with the children?

We have never sat them down and said we are gay, but we don't keep it a secret. Because they came to us so young, they have just been used to growing up with two dads, so it has never been an issue. We have read books to them that have stories about two dads.

How do you explain the children's pasts to them?

We have always explained to them that there has to be a mum and dad to have a baby. We have a personal story for both of them about how they came into the world and why they were adopted. We say they have a mummy but that she couldn't look after them, so a judge decided that they should be looked after by someone else and they were chosen by two dads. They seem to accept this for now.

You can only explain what is age-appropriate, but as they get older, we will explain more.

We have letterbox contact with Josephine's mother three times a year. We tried with Finlay's mother, arranging meetings before the adoption, but she failed to turn up four times and doesn't write. We have get-togethers with his siblings – as he is the youngest of 15, they have to wear name badges when they all attend. The oldest is 24.

How do you feel about not being a birth parent?

It has made no difference in terms of our love for them. We are not genetically related and don't look like each other, but we are so familiar with them now. It was weird when they first arrived as it seemed like an arranged marriage, but I believe you can learn to love someone. In the past, I mourned the loss of not having birth children but I haven't got any misgivings now and I wouldn't have considered sperm donation or surrogacy – we don't have to create "mini-mes". Families come in all shapes and sizes and I'm very happy with mine.

What are some of the emotional and behavioural issues you have experienced?

Our daughter can be a drama queen with magnified feelings of injustice. I tend to cuddle her and let her cry but sometimes you have to tell her to get over it. She can say things like: 'You've ruined my life', over something small.

Josephine became jealous when Finlay arrived. She told the social worker, who we are seeing about the third adoption, that the day Finlay arrived was the worst day of her life. She said: 'You promised me a baby and he was nearly walking'. She obviously expected something different. Josephine regressed when Finlay arrived, wanting dummies and to be fed from a bottle but only at home, not out of the house. I think she'll be quite a challenging teenager.

Finlay is more docile and compliant. If you ask him to put a coat on, he will say, yes, which one, whereas Josephine will say, no, I wore that one yesterday. As long as Finlay is watered, fed and warm, he seems quite content. Josephine will complain about food and demand a surprise if I'm travelling abroad on business. She'll say: 'I know you can get Ugg boots in China'. The surprise will be that she isn't getting Ugg boots!

What advice would you give about managing routines, boundaries, rewards and sanctions?

In terms of sanctions, we give warnings, then time out and then if they carry on there will be a consequence, such as not being able to go on a planned trip. You have to stick to the consequences and present a united front. Our daughter knows how far she can push it but she is not manipulative or spiteful.

We tried a reward chart, but one day Josephine ripped it up, saying she didn't want it any more.

We allow them to watch half an hour of television a day. They don't have a TV in their rooms and we don't allow them to watch the one downstairs while they eat. We don't have satellite television or any Nintendo consoles. Obviously, the pressure to get these things will increase as they get older. They can watch a DVD as a special treat.

In terms of food, we just say, if you don't eat your main course, you don't get pudding. We don't have any pre-packaged food. We make our own lasagna, pizzas, chicken casseroles, salmon and garlic mashed potato. Josephine would kill for fish fingers! They like quite sophisticated things like olives and anchovies. We don't allow any fizzy drinks and always have water on the table. We have been to McDonald's once. If we go out they are allowed to have apple juice. My theory is whatever you put in, has to come out in poo or behaviour.

We don't let them have school dinners. I make them chicken or cheese wraps and homemade banana cake. When they come home they can have biscuits and fruit as a snack. There is always fruit available. They particularly like grapes.

Have you had to deal with attachment issues?

They can be a bit ambivalent with people whom we see often, and then all over people whom we hardly see. We have had to deal with it but sometimes you need to ask, is it their age or because they have been adopted? You can risk falling into a trap of over-diagnosing.

What has been your experience of holidays?

My advice is don't go to a hotel – sharing a room is a nightmare. Obviously, it depends on your budget, but we found cruises are great – there's loads to do on a cruise. We have been on one around the Norwegian Fjords and another around the Caribbean. We also go to our house abroad where we all have our own rooms and a pool. You can sit outside when they have gone to bed and have adult time.

We also went on a driving holiday around California and another in South Africa. We sometimes go away for weekends, renting a cottage in the countryside. We are going to the Far East this summer. We try to get away three times a year. Holidays are a great way of making them see how other children live. I want to take them to India and Cambodia to show them children living on the streets.

What about pursuing hobbies/activities together?

They like camping, walking on the beach, taking the dog out and skateboarding.

How has it been with your friends and family?

Our parents have been great. However, as we are older parents, our parents, in turn, are even older and I wouldn't ask them to babysit late at night. One set lives an hour away and the other about three hours away.

We ask friends in the neighbourhood to babysit. We have lived here for 17 years so the neighbours are very friendly.

We also belong to a lesbian and gay adoption group, which is a great support. We have monthly meetings and go away for weekends with them. I never thought I would go camping, I was more used to five-star hotels – children change your life in more ways than one! We also belong to New Family Social, a lesbian and gay adoption and fostering network. We have been camping with NFS too. It is great for the kids to see other families with two dads or two mums.

What has it been like dealing with schools?

They've been great. We have always worn our hearts on our sleeves. When we shopped around for schools, our opening gambit was, 'We are a gay couple, who have adopted children. What is your policy on inclusion?'

Both children go to a local state school and it has been absolutely brilliant. The school has been very proactive in supporting us as a gay couple. We haven't experienced any negativity and they have been very careful with their language, for example, remembering to write letters to "Dear parents and carers".

Our daughter has been kept with the same class for three years, which is great as we don't have to repeat explanations.

What has been your experience of the legal system?

After a lot of pressure we have managed to change the names on the children's passports. We also had a battle getting child benefit – we were told by one official that they normally give it to the mother as dads spend it down the pub!

Have you experienced any homophobia?

I've had older mums looking at me while I was giving one of the babies a bottle as if I should be breast-feeding. I think the first health visitor came round too often. I don't think she would have done if one of us were a woman. She seemed to imply that one of us must take the more female role in our relationship. She also asked who was going to sit our daughter on the toilet.

You hear the words "poofter" and "gay" in the playground. I told a boy off the other day for using the words "poofter" and told him I was a so-called "poofter".

What advice would you like to give to social workers?

You need to be more transparent. You also need to make sure you would ask a heterosexual man the same questions as you ask a homosexual man. Don't make us jump through more hoops than straight men or women. Be supportive of gay and lesbian adopters.

And to schools?

Use the right language. We are in the twenty-first century. Say, "Dear parents and carers". They tend to be very clued up about ethnic minorities but not as supportive of other minorities.

And your final words of advice to prospective adopters?

It is not for the faint-hearted. It's like a very, very long pregnancy. From the initial inquiry to the approval process took us two years. When you go on the five-day preparation course, social workers paint a very bleak picture, which puts a lot of people off.

I now help out on preparation courses. I go in all smiles. We are both very positive about our experience, hence going for a third child. Kids will always have baggage but that is part of life.

Write a list of reasons why you want to do it. There is usually one person in the relationship who wants to do it more than the other – ask yourselves why. Ask your family and friends if they can visualise you with a child. Be realistic. Try not to have rose-tinted glasses. It is life-changing and mind-blowing but preparation is everything.

2   Menna and Gwen

Menna, 58, a full-time mum, and Gwen, 45, an academic, fostered Joe, a boy with moderate learning disabilities, when he was seven. After fostering him for three years, they decided to adopt him 18 months ago. He is now 11. They are all white British and live together in Wales.

Menna tells their story with some additional thoughts from Gwen.

Why did you decide to foster?

I had never thought I would be a mother again, as I have a birth child who is 38 and two grandchildren. Gwen and I had a discussion about having a child earlier in our relationship but decided not to. We were quite nervous about bringing up a boy but now we have our own little prince!

We had talked about fostering for a while but as we both worked full-time we thought it too scary a proposition. But when Gwen got a new job the time seemed right, and I gave up work to start fostering. We fostered through a private agency and said we were happy to foster any child from birth to 18. On the checklist that you have to fill in to say which disabilities, etc, you could manage, we ticked yes to everything. Gwen had worked with older people with learning disabilities and felt confident.

We did some short-term and respite fostering to begin with to get into the swing of it. We had one boy for six months and a few children for respite – very short-term care to give regular carers a break – and a couple of emergency placements. We fostered a 13-year-old boy who was a real Jack-the-lad. He parented his parents and was always worried about them. I took him to the beach one day and he started running around, sliding on the sand dunes, and his face changed from that of a hard man to a boy. He was happy and relaxed, doing age-appropriate stuff – this made me so happy. When we started fostering, we wanted to feel that at some point a child would look back and think 'My carers treated me alright, showed me some respect'. I think that boy will be able to do that.

After our experience of short-term fostering, we felt ready for a long-term placement.

How were you matched?

Soon after this experience, Joe came up as a possible placement. He had a brother and a sister and we were being considered for him and his younger brother. However, because of their needs, they were all placed separately but in homes near to each other.

We had a visit from Joe's social worker and our own and a lengthy discussion about both boys. All three children were in a family assessment centre with their mother and father. After a week, their father was told to leave due to inappropriate behaviour towards the children and staff, but their mother stayed for 12 weeks. Social Services knew the children would be very hard to place so they decided people could come and meet them first. We spent two weekends at the centre. I've never met such damaged children before. They had suffered such abuse and neglect. They had done nothing in their lives. They had no toys and had never been to a park. Joe was seven and still in nappies day and night.

Joe liked being sung to and watching washing machines going round. He would do that all day if you let him. It was very daunting. If anyone said no to him, he would rip his clothes and urinate and soil himself. At the same time, he was so desperate for love. He would sit on our laps and get us to sing to him. He would cling to us.

During the first weekend at the assessment centre, we gave him a bath and put him to bed. He couldn't speak very well but he asked if he would see us again. Then he burst into tears and clung to me. We decided then that we would do the best we could for him. We went back for another weekend visit and arranged to bring him home the following week.

What was it like when Joe first moved in?
We had three months of sheer hell. He had no attention span at all. He didn't know how to play. He clung to me like a leech. He must have asked one hundred times a day, 'Are you going to hurt me?' If I went to the loo, he would be hysterical, saying, 'Are you being hurt in there?' We talked to the social worker and agreed that he could come into the bathroom with me. Safer caring policies had to go out of the window. He would sit on our laps and we would read to him in bed. We would record all our decisions and discuss them with social workers.

Luckily, he went to bed at 7pm and slept well, but he would then be up at the crack of dawn. We were constantly trying to entertain him and do things constructively but you would get something like Play-Doh out and it would last about three seconds. He would eat his clothes, books and wreck things. The one thing he liked was watching TV. Our social worker said let him watch it sometimes, otherwise you will go mad.

He was so demanding and needy but it was balanced out by his affection.

What about his education?
The education authority was appalling. Joe came to us in September and he was only given a place at school in the week before Christmas. Initially,

it was left up to the social worker but then we thought if this was our child we wouldn't let the situation continue so long, so we got in touch with the local councillor but still nothing happened. Eventually, we got the number of the Director of Education and harassed him until Joe was given a place. They didn't have a spare Learning Support Assistant (LSA), which was part of the delay, but when he eventually started he loved it. Things are one hundred times better now. He has had the same LSA since he began at the school.

He is just beginning to learn how to play with other children. Before, he would keep himself separate. He has just started secondary school and we are worried that he won't get enough support. We have been told that he is only going to get 15 hours but we are going to make sure he gets a full-time LSA. You have to be very proactive with their education.

What other support have you had?

We got him therapy from early on. We knew a fantastic play therapist. We have never called it therapy but he seemed to twig straight away that it was a safe place for him to talk, which was separate from us. He's been really brave. The therapist gives him the opportunity to change the subject but he always sticks with it. If a subject comes up with us, for example, his birth parents or his behaviour, that he doesn't want to talk about, he'll say, 'I'll talk to Ciara about it'. Joe is quite reluctant to talk to us about the past although he has made some disclosures. He says he's flushed his parents down the toilet with poo on their heads.

He also has huge problems with saying sorry. One time in therapy, he asked why he should say sorry as his parents hurt him and never said sorry.

Have you had any life story work done with Joe?

Joe had some life story work which was written by a social work assistant based on an account by someone in the office who had met his parents. It is unspeakably awful. It doesn't address why Joe was taken into care. There is loads of stuff in there about how lovely his parents were, which is blatantly not true. His parents were constantly evicted and even banned from the local supermarket. If Joe could read it and reflect on it, he would think I must be mad, I can remember them locking me up and hurting me. Any normal person would have been scared by his father.

We have a story that we tell him about his past, which we used to tell him every night, but now he doesn't need it so much so we only tell it when he asks. We used to say, there was this lovely boy called Joe, who lived with his parents. We use their first names and say they weren't nice to him. Then a teacher noticed you weren't happy and she talked to Social Services and they found you a family to make you happy. Sometimes, he asks us to repeat the story and we use it if we need to introduce some change.

The first child we fostered also had this rose-tinted life story book, which described his mother as wonderful and gave no reasons why he was in care. He was so badly damaged psychologically that I suspect he may have a serious personality disorder. We don't believe you should gloss over things. He had come to us as an emergency because his carer had died suddenly. We assumed Social Services would be organising therapy for him but you should never assume they know what they are doing.

What is the best thing you have achieved?
Seeing the difference in our boy – we know he has achieved this because of us being completely dedicated to him and putting his needs first.

What advice would you give about managing challenging behaviour?
You need to praise the behaviour you want to see and try to ignore the behaviour you don't want to see. For example, if Joe is playing a computer game very loudly, you have to praise him in the minute when he is being quiet.

Start out with very firm boundaries. You can relax them later but it is harder to introduce them later on. The first four to six weeks was like a boot camp. It was incredibly hard but we praised him and gave him chocolate buttons as rewards. His sanction was sitting on a step in the living room. He used to sit there and scream, bite his arms and wet himself. We would have a big cuddle afterwards and explain why he was sanctioned.

He was so uncontrollable to start with. He would fling himself about. The only thing that could calm him down would be going for a drive but you couldn't stop anywhere.

We had to be very strict about television as he would want to watch it all day. We started out saying no TV until 4pm. Now we let him watch on weekend mornings so that we can have a bit of a lie-in.

You need to treat children at their emotional age and allow them to regress. We treated Joe like a baby as he had never had a real babyhood. We would wrap him in a blanket and play "Rock-a-bye-baby", pretend he had a bottle, read him baby books and draw "Round and round the garden" on his hands. We gradually moved on to more age-appropriate activities but damaged children won't reach their chronological age unless you allow them to regress first.

We would generally work on one behaviour at a time until it improved and then move on to the next one, but you have to be a bit relaxed about some things.

He went through a long period of peeing on the floor in the living room. We told him off and we put a sign on the wall with a picture saying pee on the toilet, not on the carpet. That seemed to work eventually.

He is also very bad at staying by our side if we go out. If you are looking at a street stall, he'll be off before you know it. You have to be on the ball all the time. You have to plan everything and tell him what the rewards and sanctions will be in advance, for example, saying that he will have an icecream if he stays with us.

A lot of the difficulties are caused by neglect and trauma rather than his learning difficulties.

I would say to anyone trying to manage challenging behaviour that you also need to retain a sense of humour.

Have you had any disappointments?
As we live in a rural area, we don't get many placements. As we foster

through an agency, local authorities will only place children here if they are desperate. It comes down to money all the time.

We were quite happy with Joe and would have continued supporting him through our agency but the local authority decided to put him up for adoption. They advertised him in *Be My Parent*. They had asked us if we wanted to adopt and initially we said no. We thought as long as he had enough time for the transition, he would be alright. However, the therapist said leaving us would cause him more damage than anything that had happened to him in the past. He was so attached to us, trusted us and was happy. He called our house, his 'happy ever after house'. By then we loved him and he was so much part of our lives, we decided adoption was the right thing to do.

How did the adoption process go?

It was supposed to be fast-tracked but it still took 18 months. Things move so slowly, not helped by the social worker going on sick leave. We were also negotiating an adoption allowance and money for his therapy, which all took a long time. Gwen was made redundant during this time. We wanted to make sure we had enough money coming in so that I didn't need to work, so I could be here for Joe when he came home from school and take him to clubs, etc.

They eventually agreed to give us a weekly allowance, which was a third less than we were receiving before. Damaged children are more expensive – he is still in nappies at night but they don't soak it all up so he has to have a change of bedding and clothes every night. He is a very messy eater and a bit wobbly so he often goes through several sets of clothes in the day. We have gone through two washing machines. He also fiddles with electronic things and breaks them, including a TV, two computers and numerous CD players.

Have you experienced any homophobia?

There are some people in the village who think we are "an abomination" and that no child should be near us, but most have been supportive – they look out for Joe. We get a lot of positive feedback from people who can see him developing.

In the local secondary school, they were discussing lesbian and gay adoption and a girl spoke up in class and said we have a lesbian couple in our village and they are fantastic.

When we first applied to foster, one of the agencies we approached clearly had a problem with us, but the agency we chose is fine with us.

We don't really see our sexuality as such a big thing as we did when we were younger. We are completely settled and have been together for 19 years, so now it is just a part of us, almost incidental.

It might have been different if Joe didn't have a learning disability. He calls me Mammy and Gwen Mum but he doesn't understand the concept of Mother's Day. He asked if I was a mum and I said, yes I'm your mum.

Our first placement was a boy who was from a born-again Christian family. He had a very strange attitude to women. He was so wrapped up in that, I don't think he saw us as lesbians. We didn't think it would have worked out as a long-term placement.

What have you learned about yourself?
I'm more impatient than I thought I was.

Have your families been supportive?
They have been fantastic. When we were first thinking about adoption I rang Gwen's parents to ask what they thought and they said it would make no difference to them, Joe was already part of the family.

When we first started fostering, my daughter was a bit wary. It has taken her a long time to come round to the idea. Over the last six months, things have become better. I think the problem was that we never sat down and talked about it with her, it just happened.

And your friends?
The friends we have now are the ones who have been supportive. Others we don't see any more. We went to visit one set of friends and Joe broke something. They were furious and didn't show any interest in him.

You really need friends and family to be supportive. We can't take him to see friends easily because it is very unsettling for him although he has become fond of some of them. It is always better for people to visit us at home.

You need to think about what you do with your friends now and how that will change.

We have also met new friends – other parents of children with disabilities – who we wouldn't have met otherwise. We now have a good support group around us. We joined an adoption support group and went to one meeting in the summer holidays. Joe's sister is adopted and her adoptive mother comes to the meetings.

Is there any other birth family contact?

Unfortunately, we don't have a good relationship with his brother's carers and they don't like him seeing Joe.

Joe loves his sister and they meet up every six weeks. Their relationship has improved as time has gone on – they didn't really have a relationship when he was first adopted as she was still a baby. Her adoptive parents are very keen to maintain contact.

We write to Joe's birth parents once a year.

What impact has adoption had on your life?

It has been totally exhausting. We don't have the quality time that we used to have. We do get respite as part of the adoption plan but it took over a year to sort it out. We get 18 days a year paid for by direct payments.

We have support workers who come and stay here. Ideally, we would like respite once a month but we don't get that due to the difficulties of recruiting support workers. When we first had respite, we just used to sleep, but it is not as bad as that now. He used to need two carers all the time.

And on your finances?

Things have changed because of Gwen being made redundant and she is now a student again. We have gone from a good salary to living on benefits, a bursary and the adoption allowance.

You need to allow for one of you to stay at home, at least during the first year, if not two. Joe would not have progressed as much as he has if we had both had to work. You can't put looked after children in day care, they need your full-time attention.

Would you adopt or foster again?

We wouldn't adopt now because of our ages but we would if we were younger. We are talking about fostering again, possibly another disabled child, as we know we can care for disabled children and give them a good life. That would also be a better fit for Joe. We would only do short-term or respite with the agency or local authority.

We have built an extension on the strength of planning for more children.

How do you feel about not being Joe's birth parent?

Gwen says: 'I never wanted birth children anyway, never had a biological urge. I think it's a very heterosexual thing to have an obsession with blood relations. If you love a child it shouldn't make any difference if you are related or not, love is love.'

We never expected to feel such love for a child. We are both besotted with him. To know his background and to see how he is so resilient is amazing – we call him "sunshine Joe". I think we had more access to information than you get now about his parents. We also met both his parents, old teachers and his previous Learning Support Assistant (LSA).

I can't describe it but I feel differently towards my daughter and Joe. I was besotted with her but I think your relationship with an adopted child is different. They are also at very different stages in their lives. I think you feel extra protective towards an adopted child because of their background.

What has been your experience of holidays?

Gwen adds: 'I find holidays exhausting. I get ratty because I expect some relaxation but Joe wants full-time attention. I have to see it as being on duty and think, 'this is Joe's holiday, don't expect a break'.

Joe finds it difficult to be on holiday and is generally unsettled by being away from home. The first time was in Gwen's parents' caravan and he was terrified. He wouldn't even go in it when we arrived.

We also went to stay with a friend and one of us ended up singing him to sleep, saying 'Joe is safe now, safe in his cosy bed, safe from all harm' for up to an hour.

Some holidays have been a complete nightmare. We decided to get a campervan so he would be in a familiar space. The first couple of times were difficult but now he's settled.

We've taken him away a lot – three times abroad, to bed and breakfasts and to friends, and I think this was initially too ambitious. I would suggest not going on holiday until a child is settled and then just doing short trips.

Gwen adds: 'When we went to a hotel in Majorca, I was feeling very tired. I remember playing with him in the pool and feeling very tired and disgruntled. I just wanted some time to read a newspaper but to be honest if I got three minutes, I was lucky.'

What activities does Joe like?

Joe loves swimming. Mind you, the first time he screamed blue murder. I put him on a mat and sang to him to soothe him. By the end of the session, he loved it. When we were in Lanzarote for a week, he taught himself to swim by taking off the armbands and just swimming. He was in the pool for eight hours a day.

His support worker takes him swimming. He can now do front crawl and has got medals in gymnastics and trophies for coming first in the vault. He came second in a floor routine in a whole of Wales competition.

He won a national artwork competition three years running in his class of disabled children. He has learned to ride a bike, which is a huge achievement because his balance and co-ordination are not so good. He has learned to stand on one leg recently.

We took him to Beavers but all these things need a gradual introduction and one-to-one support. Eventually, they said he was too old for Beavers but unfortunately Cubs was too advanced for him.

I think it's a good idea to keep kids as busy as possible, try any activity and encourage them. Joe goes to an athletics club on Monday and an art club. If he misbehaves at the group, we persist as the whole point is for him to learn to socialise.

What advice would you give to social workers?
They need to recognise that we are professionals with experience.

Safer caring has its place but it can get in the way of a child's development. Children need to build a sense of appropriate touch and holding to feel safe and loved. You have to use your common sense and talk about what is the best way of being for the child. Don't just have a blanket policy.

And to schools?
Make sure everyone knows about the children and their triggers. Teachers should have basic training about looked after children and trauma and gain an understanding of attachment disorder. Children are not naughty, they are just traumatised. There are lots of implications of attachment disorder on learning.

And to policy-makers?
Pay foster carers and adopters a decent amount of money. Surely a cost/benefit analysis would show that it is better to spend the money on children in care so they won't end up in prison.

Family courts should also look at taking away children sooner.

What advice would you give to people thinking about fostering or adoption?
Try short-term to start with to see how you cope. I always say imagine the worst case scenario of a child you know and then imagine it ten times worse. You will be getting a severely damaged child, so you need to think about

how you would cope.

You both have to be totally on board and committed and singing from the same hymn sheet in terms of discipline.

Be prepared for anything and get therapy for the child. However well adjusted children appear, they are damaged. Try to get the local authority to pay but if not, pay for it yourself. Obviously, it will depend on the child but they will need therapy from time to time as they grow up.

Adopters should think about older children – don't hang out for a baby, you can get so much pleasure from older children. Although Joe was seven, we still went through many of the pleasures of baby and toddlerhood – paddling pools, water play, finger painting, first trips to the park and swimming pool. You also have fewer years of exhaustion with older children!

It's love that children thrive on, not necessarily having heterosexual parents. Lesbians and gay men make just as good parents.

And finally . . . pick your friends carefully, keep a sense of humour, make sure you have time for yourself, get kids to bed at a reasonable hour, apply for an adoption allowance, and don't be too proud to say if it's not working.

3 Anthony and Christos

Anthony, 49, white British, is a retired actor. His partner, Christos, 40, white Greek, is a head chef. They initially fostered two brothers, Simon and Josh, when they were aged seven and five. They arrived as an emergency placement but lived with Anthony and Christos for three years. Social Services then decided to put the boys up for adoption. Anthony and Christos couldn't let them go, so adopted the boys themselves three years ago. The boys are now aged 13 and 11. They all live together in London.

Anthony tells their story.

Why did you decide to foster?

We decided to foster to see if we were suited to looking after children. It seemed a less permanent option, although this never turned out to be the case. We made a decision quite early on that any child who came to stay in our house could stay as long as they needed to. When Social Services said our two boys were going to be put up for adoption, we couldn't bear to see them go. In the end, for us there has not been much difference between fostering and adoption.

What were the children like when they first moved in?

They had lots of problems and were behind developmentally. They were still in nappies and drinking from baby's bottles. They wouldn't eat properly. It was like having two toddlers. They didn't get on with each other and were scared and mistrustful. They had statements of special need at school and the authorities thought they might be autistic. One teacher told us she had to teach them to sit on a chair before she could start teaching them.

What has been your greatest achievement?

I think it is what the boys have achieved, turning their lives around from the hell of being taken away from their mother in the middle of the night to live with two strangers, to becoming trusting and loving and part of a safe, secure and happy family.

Have there been any surprises?

I sometimes wish I hadn't done it and that surprises me. I have a fear of doing the wrong thing and having a negative impact. I'm often not sure if I have taken the right approach. It is probably a similar feeling to birth parents, wondering if you can handle situations, but then I look at the boys and I love them so much.

Did you do anything to mark the difference between fostering and adoption?

When we adopted the boys we had a civil partnership to make our legal status easier. We had a party afterwards but called it our adoption party for the boys. I gave a speech saying I thought I would never have a family of my own and how that had made me sad. I loved being a child and part of a big family with three sisters and two brothers and I wanted to have a family of my own. I'm so glad we have been given this opportunity.

What difference do you think it has made being a gay foster carer/ adopter?

I think it has been harder for the children at school with some name-calling and some parents not wanting their children to come here. There haven't been many incidents and the schools are very good. I guess children always find reasons to pick on other kids. It doesn't seem to have held them back. Simon had his statement removed after a year as he was flourishing at school.

I don't think it is about us being gay as neither of us is effeminate, but Simon went through a phase after a year of living with us of wanting everything to be pink and girly. A straight friend of ours said her son did the same thing at the age of two, which is probably the appropriate age for this sort of phase. However, we didn't stop our son as he hadn't had a chance to be like that when it was appropriate. He grew out of it but it was important to let him go through that stage.

What have you learned about yourself?
To be more patient and to use elements of the way you were parented that you liked but to try not to repeat the things you didn't like. I think it's a natural progression, you have to inspect closely everything you do or say. Sometimes I lose my temper but it makes me look at the way I behave, about what is right and wrong. You look at the world in a different way and develop a philosophy about life.

Overall, it is very positive. I'm calmer now. Some things don't seem to matter so much because there are more important things to think about. I used to be a glass half empty sort of person. I think it has made me a much better person. How much I love them is amazing, I don't think my heart can cope sometimes.

What sort of contact do you have with their birth family?
Simon and Josh's mother wasn't intentionally unkind to them, and she is their mother and part of their lives, so we include her as part of our family. We phone her every month and send postcards. She sees them three times a year. At first, it was really upsetting but now contact is part of our lives.

How do you feel about not being a birth parent?
Actually, I am a birth parent, although I didn't have any involvement in my daughter's upbringing. I had a girlfriend when I was 17 and she became pregnant and emigrated to Australia with her family and went on to marry

someone else. When my daughter turned 18, we traced each other and got to know each other. She is now 30 and has a son, my grandson, who is the same age as our younger son. She and my grandson are living with us for now. She lived with us previously, for a year, when my grandson was aged four.

I don't really think about my sons not being birth children. Their birth father died before they moved in with us and they wanted to find where his ashes were buried. Once we had managed to find the garden of remembrance, Simon and Josh were more at peace. We consider that they have three dads.

What effect has fostering and adoption had on your own relationship?
At first it was very negative. For the first two years my partner was working a lot as he runs a restaurant, so I felt like a single parent. The children used to call him 'that other man'. Christos was working so much and I was so exhausted, I'm ashamed to say we used to row a lot in the beginning. We apologised to the kids and showed them that we were working things out. We are now in a stronger place – things are great and we talk about everything. You need to be able to talk about your feelings.

You have to make time for each other and get babysitters so you can get out. We were able to do this once the boys were more secure.

How have your friends and family been?
They have mainly been really supportive. Our families embraced the children from the start. My family was very happy when we decided to adopt Simon and Josh. Children are really important in my family. My parents spend time with the boys, talking to them, complimenting them and telling them stories. Simon and Josh both felt very comfortable with them from the start.

Our close friends have been very supportive. A few friends disappeared as soon as the children came along and some were nervous at the beginning.

Have you experienced any homophobia?
Nearly all the social workers have been positive. We had a couple of problems with one who was taken off our case. Sometimes you can get problems with people's religious beliefs. We also had a problem with a doctor who didn't

seem comfortable with us – he asked where my wife was so I explained my situation. When I went for my medical to be approved as an adopter he tested me for HIV and said the results would take two weeks. My partner went to a different doctor, didn't have to take an HIV test and returned with the health certificate that day. As soon as someone does something inappropriate, I put my complaint in writing and nip it in the bud. In this case I wrote to the General Medical Council and the doctor apologised. I also went to a different doctor to get my certificate more quickly.

What advice would you give about managing routines, boundaries, rewards, sanctions, television, computer time, etc?

Now Simon and Josh are 13 and 11, some of the boundaries are a bit more blurred, but at the beginning, mealtimes and bedtimes were always at set times. It is really important to be consistent. We made lots of rules and I was quite strict. We had reward charts for going to the toilet, brushing teeth and other routines. They liked getting stars. We didn't label it as "being good" but behaving in certain acceptable ways.

I had to reassure them that it was my job to take care of them and make sure they were safe, and that was why we had rules. They seemed to flourish because they had never had this sort of structure before.

Saturday morning is when they have to do homework and we usually have one activity at the weekend, such as bowling or going to the cinema. After lunch we have quiet time when we read for an hour. We instigated this as they didn't seem to be reading and I love reading.

We used to set a timer so they had half an hour each of television or whatever activity they needed to share. Now we don't have set amounts of time that they can watch TV or be on the computer, but we tell them when we think they have had enough.

One of our rules is that they have to try everything we give them to eat but if they don't like it, they don't have to eat it.

Another rule is no hitting. One time, Simon hit Josh very hard and Social Services found out. It was very worrying and we had to reassure them that it wouldn't happen again. It hasn't happened since.

When they do something wrong, we say we have to talk and they have to sit down with us and discuss at length the problem and how we are going to sort it out. We explain why it isn't nice and ask them how they would feel if someone did it to them. Sometimes we get them to draw things to help them express their feelings or actions.

However, there are times when all the explaining in the world doesn't get through. Once, Simon was being violent at school and they were threatening to exclude him. We were going to Butlins that weekend as a family. We told him he had to stop being violent but he still threw some chairs across the school dining hall. Luckily, he didn't get excluded but Josh and Christos went to Butlins without us. Simon was very upset about it and we talked about his behaviour and why he had been denied the treat. It was hard but I'm glad we followed through and he learned not to do it again.

Have you had holidays together?

At first the boys were very fearful, so we had to explain a lot to them before we went away to prepare them, telling them about where we were going, the timings and how we were getting there, so that they felt secure. In fact the first time we went on a plane the children loved it and they took to skiing straight away.

Now they love going on trips. As Christos is Greek we often go to Greece for holidays. We have also been to Australia, which they loved. We went to Iceland to see the Northern Lights. We also go up to the north of England to see my family.

What about hobbies and activities together?

Initially, just going to the park was an adventure. When they first came to us they couldn't even climb on a climbing frame or go on a swing because they were so fearful. They didn't have very much co-ordination. Now Simon loves climbing.

They were also terrified of swimming at first and Josh wouldn't let go of us in the water. He used to cry before we went to the pool and I sometimes felt mean taking him, but by the end of each session he was loving it. You have to persevere with things.

We have tried to introduce them to as much as possible including football club, drumming and cookery lessons. Sometimes they don't want to go at first so you have to make them try a few times and then if they really don't like it, give up.

Have you had to deal with attachment issues?

Simon wouldn't come near us to start with. Josh was very clingy and was trying to get in the way of his brother, so that made Simon step back even more. Simon found adults scary. He remembered being there when his father died, which was very traumatic. He used to say that he didn't like anyone or love anyone, not even his brother.

And with sibling rivalry?

Simon and Josh used to push each other away but now they are very close. It is really important to comment on their good behaviour, when they are playing together well, rather than just noticing when they are fighting – that way they get the attention for the behaviour you want to see, but it can be hard to remember because you are so relieved when it is quiet.

How have you discussed your sexuality with the children?

We have just answered questions when they have come up. When they first arrived, they asked if we were brothers and we told them we were partners. They then asked if we sleep in the same bed and whether we wear clothes in bed. When we had the adoption party after our civil partnership they asked if it meant that we were married.

On another occasion, one of them came home from school saying, 'My friend says gay people dance with the devil'. I just laughed it off, saying we like dancing but not with the devil.

There has never been a question about sexuality that we haven't been able to answer honestly.

How have you answered questions about their sexuality?

They are very open and ask questions about puberty, such as wet dreams and even girls' periods. We use humour if we can and try not to make it embarrassing. We have also talked to them about sex being about emotions and feelings, not just the physical act.

What advice would you give to social workers?

I think they need to be more relaxed about the safer caring rules. We were told not to sit on their bed to read a bedtime story, to put a cushion between us if they wanted a cuddle, etc. The safer caring part of the preparation course made me feel fearful, although I can see that they obviously want to keep children safe. However, children have already had their lives broken apart and they don't need you pushing them away.

The children have now been with us for six years and in the last year they have started coming in and jumping on our bed. That is absolutely fine with us. Our 13-year-old still snuggles up when we are watching TV.

They might seem a bit old to be doing that but they are catching up on things they couldn't do when they were younger. I think it would be bad if we rejected them. When we were fostering we wouldn't have been allowed to let them come into our room without knocking first, but all children want to run in and jump on your bed and it seems natural.

And final words for people thinking about fostering or adopting?

Really make sure you want to do it. Be absolutely certain. Once you take a child into your life if you then reject them, the damage you would do to them would be awful. You need to decide that whatever problems occur you are going to be there for them.

If you really do want to do it, you will never regret it. When they brought those two little boys to our door, they were in such a state and really scared. Now when I look back, it breaks my heart. I see them as my children and can't bear to think of them going through that. They will always be our children and we will always be their dads and that feels right.

4

Leah and Jane

Leah, 43, Eastern European, and Jane, 46, white British, adopted Luke, an Eastern European boy. He moved in when he was six months old and was formally adopted when he was 11 months old. He is now six-and-a-half. Leah is a marketing manager and Jane has been a "stay at home" mum but is about to start work as a teaching assistant at a school for boys with behavioural and emotional issues. They live in the South West of England.

Leah and Jane applied to adopt again a few years ago but gave up after 18 months because social workers couldn't find them a suitable match. They have now gone through the approval process for a third time. At the time of interview they were one week away from the approval panel. This time they want a three-year-old so there is not too big an age gap between the children. Leah and Jane don't mind if the next child is a girl or a boy but Luke wants a brother.

Leah tells their story with some additional comments from Jane.

Why did you decide to adopt?

We had been together 10 years and when we explored the possibility of having a child, we felt we wanted to make it as equal as possible with both of us having parental rights. We thought about IVF but felt adoption was the right choice for us. Jane's parents had also fostered for a while so we had an understanding of the kind of kids who needed homes.

What would you say to someone thinking of adopting?

Go for it, but be prepared for an absolute rollercoaster of a ride and that's before you have a child placed with you. The assessment process is soul-searching and quite thorough.

It has been fantastic and absolutely the right thing for us to do. It can be really tough and for a relationship it can be quite a make or break situation.

Jane adds: 'It is the best thing we've done. I can't imagine our lives without our boy now. It's fantastic. Like all parents, he has completely changed our lives.'

What preparation did you have before adopting?

The social workers said we needed some childcare experience so we worked as respite foster carers for about four weekends. However, we found it too difficult. The social worker plonked this child on us, didn't give us any idea of his routine, and picked him up three days later. It was so painful. We realised that complex needs were too much for us. It is important to know your limitations. It was a good eye-opener but I'm glad we didn't do it for too long.

What was the legal aspect of adoption like?

Three months before our formal adoption of Luke, the law changed allowing couples to adopt legally. We were one of the first gay or lesbian couples to adopt equally. This was great because we wanted equality between us. The judge was really lovely, very positive, and we had a wonderful day.

What do you think is the best thing you have achieved?

Being matched with Luke. When you are going through the adoption process they tell you not to expect a baby and they prepare you for having a child with complex needs. We have been extremely lucky in getting Luke when he was so young, so he didn't have some of the complex issues that children coming into care later on might have. We also experienced parenting a baby – all the good stuff – all the sleepless nights and all the rest of it. To know him from six months old has been a fantastic opportunity.

Can you describe Luke and his background?

An all-round lovely chap, a normal six-year-old. He likes to talk about football, and is obsessed with the Wii, computer games – all that kind of stuff.

Jane adds: 'He is very handsome, funny, confident, cocky, bright, a good boy, well behaved most of the time, has his moments but he's bound to, he's not really challenging.'

Luke's mother is Eastern European. We don't know much about his father at all. She came to our local town and had him in the local hospital. He was pretty much a relinquished baby. Social Services were involved from when he was three days old.

Have there been any surprises?

I found the introductions very tough and challenging. On the day we went to meet Luke, we ended up being about an hour late because I just found it so overwhelming to think that we were going to meet the child who was going to be our son. I just couldn't get my head around it at all, I found it very difficult. Whereas before I'd found other aspects a bit easier than Jane, for example, going forward for matching and then not being matched was more painful for her.

Jane adds: 'I was surprised by the obvious homophobia from social workers. When we would ring up to say we were interested in a child who we thought would be a good match, there would be a pause while they racked their brains to think of a reason not to let us have any more information. It took three years from the time we first applied to adopt to being matched with Luke. The second time we applied to adopt, we had found a good match, but we were told the birth mother didn't want their child brought up by two women.'

In 2010, we decided to apply again and this time around we have both been surprised at how differently we have been perceived. We have already been sent children's profiles, we feel more in control. I think the world has had time to catch up with the fact that gay people are parenting. There aren't many people now who haven't seen same-sex couples with children around. I think that has become the norm. Whereas I think 10 years ago social workers thought lesbian and gay couples would only adopt kids that nobody else wanted, which often meant really challenging kids. That is not a good assumption to make, as not everyone has the skills to cope with challenging kids. Now social workers are looking for permanent families for children and it is a much more level playing field. I am really pleased about that.

What sort of child do you hope to be matched with this time around?

We would like a child aged around three, who can fit in with the kind of stuff we do as a family, such as going to the park and swimming. I think a baby this time around would be too big a gap between the child and Luke who is nearly seven.

Luke would like a boy. He wants to balance the gender make-up of our household. I think we'll probably err towards a boy but let's see what life has to bring. You don't want to be too fussy, saying blue eyes or brown hair, you just want someone who will fit in with your family. When I first started this process it was horrendous looking at all the children in the magazines because I thought I could give a home to all of them, but now we have to be realistic and think about how they would get on with Luke. He needs to get something out of it as well.

How does Luke feel about it?

He is excited.

Jane says: 'Part of the reason we applied for a third time is because he has been calling our dog his brother. He would really like a brother so that was the final push for us. In years down the line, I don't want to say we couldn't be bothered. I want to say we tried. I feel quite positive this time.'

I also think it is important to be realistic. The second time around, social workers were thinking we could cope with children with Asperger's or autism but I think you need to have a real understanding of the parenting skills required and have more time. It wouldn't be fair on Luke to be diverting so much time to a child with such special needs.

What difference do you think it's made being a lesbian couple?

When Luke was first at school, some of the other children thought he was the luckiest child ever because he had two mums. At that age, their mums are the person they want to spend more time with and often they don't have a dad around anyway. Now around six and seven, I think their currency is different. It's more about going to see *Star Wars* and rough and tumble boys' stuff. We do that and we make sure he gets time with male friends of ours, but it took us a while to adjust to that expectation. I think when he understood that he wasn't missing out, that made the difference.

Jane adds: 'I came to parenting when I was 40 and I think being an older parent helps. We have done our partying and are happy to put that behind us and can now concentrate on family life and settle down. So I think he's lucky having two older parents and two mums. Us being able to spend time with him has given him confidence and stability. I also think having experienced homophobia in our lives, we are much more open to diversity and we are bringing him up to accept everyone for who they are.'

What difference do you feel you have made to Luke's life?

If he had stayed with his birth parents, he would have lived a life of poverty and neglect. He wouldn't have had the experiences that we have given him. I think he would have been a child who rattled around the system, in and out of care and different foster homes. From what we know of his birth mother she didn't have the capacity or the lifestyle to provide a home for him. I think she did him a favour by not attempting to do that. I'm glad she gave him the chance.

Jane adds: 'We formally adopted him at the age of 11 months and I don't know of a child who has been adopted that soon. It is really rare to be adopted so young but it means he had stability from an early age and I think that's what he needed.'

What have you learned about yourselves?

Jane says: 'I think the process was really good for me, talking to the social worker about how I was parented. It was a bit like therapy. I took full advantage of it to work some stuff out. It has given me quite a lot of confidence, parenting a child and Luke doing so well. I've grown as a person. It's setting me off thinking about it. I do cry a lot! It opens you up to your emotions. I used to worry about it but now I think it's amusing. I even cry at pantomimes or if it snows – I blame the hormones!'

We have still got the same social worker who approved us, which has helped a lot. She became used to us crying. In terms of learning about myself, it is such a life-changing experience I find it hard to go back to how I viewed the world. I have changed quite significantly as a person. I connect with people very differently now on a more emotional level and see the humanity of everything. I think before I was going through life on quite a superficial level, skating through rather than getting deep into it. I could have stayed doing that and I don't think I would have noticed what I was missing out on.

What has been your experience of dealing with schools?
Jane says: 'We went into it with our sleeves rolled up. We said right from the beginning, this is our life, Luke has two mums. We were on the defensive, we didn't give anyone a chance. We said, if there is any homophobia or if anything is said we want to know about it and we will help you deal with it. I have to say so far it's been brilliant right from nursery through to his fourth year now.'

When we were first visiting schools, we went to quite a few, including a Catholic school, as I'm Catholic and Luke has been christened. We chose one that had more of a community feel. It looked like it was more liberal in its view. It had all its policies and procedures in place, had a statement about homophobia not being tolerated and had an outstanding Ofsted report. Following a meeting with the teachers, we decided this was going to work for us. We have been in every time he gets a new teacher and said he's got two mums, if there are any problems or you need our help dealing with homophobia, let us know.

Jane notes: 'There are some parents who seem to keep their distance. I think sometimes they aren't sure which one of us is which because we share the same clothes. There are some who keep themselves to themselves and they probably wouldn't be open to play dates with Luke but they are few and far between.

We sometimes get asked who had Luke and then when we say he's both of ours, they ask how that happened and we say he's adopted. Once they know that they seem to be more positive. It's like it wouldn't be OK if he'd been from a previous relationship or IVF, which is sad really. As soon as you play the adoption card people are very positive.'

What does Luke call you?

As I am Polish, he calls me Mama and he calls Jane Mummy. The same applies to names for our parents – he uses the Polish words for my parents and nanny and grandad for Jane's parents. My parents speak a little bit of Polish to him and he's got that heritage there, which I think will be good when he is more concerned about his identity as a teenager.

How supportive have your family and friends been?

Jane says: 'It's been surprising – the people who we thought wouldn't give much support, like Leah's parents, as they are Catholic, have been our biggest advocates, so that has been really nice. But some people, who were originally our referees, we never see. They thought it was lovely that we were going to adopt but then the reality is that we can't go out partying, so we drop off their radar. We have had a shift in our friendship groups. We now have more straight friends and more friends with children.

When we announced at Christmas that we were going to adopt again, we received a really positive response from friends and family. When I said don't worry, we won't burden you with anything, they said you must burden us, we want to hear the highs and lows, we want to go through this journey with you. I was surprised by that, knowing how difficult the second attempt was, so that was a great response.'

What would you say to social workers and other professionals?

Social work is really subjective. No matter how many tick boxes there are, social workers get a feel for the families and children they match. I spoke to a social worker who retired recently and she said she goes on instinct. She said, if I know who is going to be a good match, I make the boxes work. I think that was a really honest response because I think that is what happens.

I don't see the point in putting people with staunch religious views in charge of adoption and fostering placements. I'd always want to know if it would make any difference to a social worker if they were placing a child with a man and a woman or two women.

It is really important to make sure adopters have good support. Many gay men and lesbians come to adoption as a positive choice, not because other methods didn't work. We also don't come to it with the expectation of producing a child in our own image.

Other foster carers shouldn't make assumptions about gay men and lesbians. Before we adopted, we did some respite foster caring and had two girls who had been sexually abused. Their foster carer asked if we slept in the same bed. When we said yes, she said: 'That might be a problem as these two girls have been sexually abused and we don't want them to see any funny business.'

We do sleep in the same bed but most couples do, don't they? We complained to Social Services about her lack of understanding and her assumption that we would be inappropriate. She was promptly sent on an awareness course. However, she also turned out to be Luke's foster carer, so we ended up meeting her face-to-face, which was a bit awkward.

After Luke had been placed with us for a couple of months, we took him back to see her. She admitted she was reluctant about him going to two women because she'd never seen it before, but now she was glad he was placed with us because she could see how much we loved him and how well he was doing. So that was nice that we seemed to have turned that situation around. Most people come around when they know you. Unfortunately, some social workers never get to know us because they can't get past our application forms.

What difference has adoption made to your lifestyle?
Jane says: 'We used to go to expensive restaurants, plays in London and

enjoy foreign holidays. However, we soon discovered that going on an aeroplane with Luke was a nightmare. Now we go to a caravan in Cornwall and it's great, we love it. We used to go to lots of parties but we are never happier than when all three of us sit down and have our "cinema" nights, with popcorn, or we even enjoy camping in the garden.

Children make you young again. You discover everything again through their eyes. Before I might have seen snow as cold, slippery and sludgy but now I see it as great fun.'

How has adoption affected your work and finances?

Jane hasn't worked full-time or permanently since we had Luke. It was part of our adoption "bid" that one of us could stay at home and always pick him up from school. However, I was made redundant once which made life a bit of a struggle but I am now back in employment. In all honesty, if you are financially able I would advocate one of you staying at home.

How has it affected your relationship?

We had to work out our roles. I was concerned that as Jane was looking after him I would end up being like the "dad". However, you don't have to assign roles, we are just fluid about who does what.

Jane adds: 'We spend a lot of time dissecting the day, discussing what we could have done better. You find out a lot about each other through parenting.'

Have you discussed your sexuality with Luke?

We tell him that all families are different, some have mums and dads, some have two mums, some have two dads or one parent. If he was bullied it wouldn't occur to him that it was because he has two mums. We have similar conversations about adoption, explaining it to him and he says: 'I know the story. You can put the memory box away.' We are going by the beat of his drum.

How do you feel about not being a birth parent?

Jane says: 'When he first moved in, I wished I was his birth mother but now

I just think I'm incredibly lucky. I think there is an assumption that because you are genetically related you will love your children but some people don't have that capacity. Equally, I think non-birth parents have the capacity to love children just as much.'

Have you had to deal with emotional and behavioural issues?

We haven't had many difficulties. He was withdrawing from drugs when he first came to live with us and his development was quite delayed. Although he was six months, he was more like a two-month-old. He also had mild speech delay and his teeth have decayed quickly but we are hoping that his new teeth will be better. Generally, he is healthy and fit and is in the top groups for English, Maths and Science.

What advice would you give about routines, boundaries, rewards and sanctions?

I would definitely recommend getting into a routine but be prepared to change every few months and make sure you are fair. Children have got a strong sense of right and wrong. Talk to them as human beings, giving them choices – not unlimited but, for example, a choice between two options of what they wear. Only discipline if you are prepared to carry out the punishment, otherwise they will get wise to you.

Luke is quite a laid-back boy and doesn't get very angry. The down side of this can be lack of motivation to do school work. If anything upsets him he tends to withdraw. You have to ask why he is behaving in certain ways.

What has been your experience of holidays?

Get a tent – kids love camping. Our skiing holiday was a disaster as he was too young. The best holiday was a week in a caravan in Cornwall so that is why we continue to go back there. Another success was Center Parcs – anything with activities and other children.

What activities have worked well for you?

Swimming, walking the dog, Laser Quest, an action adventure game, the Wii, gardening, playing in the tree house, a punch bag, Lego, African drumming classes, jigsaws, the sandpit, making decorations for Christmas, Valentine's Day and Easter are all good fun. The Wii has a certain amount of currency in school. Some kids boast that they have one in their room and can play it all night. We don't allow him to have a TV or PC in his bedroom. He gets points for doing things around the house, homework or reading a book and can use them to spend time on the Wii.

What message would you like to give to social workers?

Don't view us as a lesbian couple. Take that off the profile. Just match us, as people, with children who would benefit from what we can offer. You need to tackle the religious social workers who object to same-sex adoption.

And to the media?

You still need to tackle stereotypical images of the family.

Which resources would you recommend?

BAAF's books, LGBT parenting groups and other people who have adopted.

And your final advice to anyone thinking of adopting?

We all have worries about our ability to parent but you've only got one life and children can play such a big part of that, you can share so much and become part of the community. It is brilliant.

And a word or two from Luke, aged six-and-a-half

I like living here, playing on the Wii, Lego and DS, going swimming and to other places.

Postscript

Jane and Leah have now been matched with a three-year-old boy who recently moved in with them.

5   Paul and Justin

Paul, 38, white British, works in advertising and
Justin, 41, is a teacher, originally from North
America. They adopted a two-and-a-half-year-old
boy, Scott, over three years ago. Previously, Scott
was living with his brother in a foster family for two
years. Paul, Justin and Scott live together in London.

Paul tells their story.

What has been your greatest achievement?

Keeping Scott alive and developing our relationship over the last three years.
You start off by meeting a child for the first time, some people say it is love
at first sight but for me, the more time I spend with him, the more I love him.
We have developed a greater understanding of each other and a greater
sense of certainty and purpose. Things that used to be massive issues are no
longer so big. This is partly down to him being older but partly down to us
knowing how to cope with his behaviour and being in a better position to

deal with it. This gives me a great feeling of achievement – creating a family life for us all.

What impact has adoption had on your lifestyle?

It is a massive change, which you need to be prepared for – there is less spontaneity, less travel and you certainly don't get upgraded on aeroplanes! However, Scott has given us a joy in our lives that we never expected to have. He has completely changed our lives. I care deeply about Scott and he loves us.

Have there been any surprises?

I'm surprised at how insanely proud I am of Scott learning to read and write – I didn't expect to be so amazed by it.

What has worked well for you?

When issues have come up, Justin and I talk about them and research ideas and solutions. I am very glad to be in a couple, I think it would be much harder as a single parent.

I also found meeting other people in similar situations very helpful in the early stages, for example, going to the New Family Social group, where you can meet other gay and lesbian adopters and foster carers. As we have bedded down as a family, I haven't felt such a need to consult others but it is good to know there are other people out there.

What difference do you think it has made being a gay adopter?

I think you soon realise that being gay has very little to do with parenting, you are so busy just getting on with everyday life. Having gay parents hasn't been a massive issue for Scott at school. He has come home saying he has got two dads, so he is clearly processing it. As far as we know, he is the only child with two dads at school. The school is very matter of fact about us being gay parents. On Mother's Day, we got a card addressed to Dad and Daddy. Justin used to teach there and is now deputy chair of governors, so he is able to oversee school policy.

You choose your friends but obviously you can't choose your children's friends and you have to get to know their friends' parents. Sometimes, I worry about how they might react when I come out to them, especially as some of them may have strong religious beliefs, but they have all been fine so far – nobody seems to have batted an eyelid.

What difference overall have you made to Scott's life?
We both really care a lot about him and want to help him to achieve his potential. I think giving him our time, love and attention has made a big difference to him. He seems very happy with us and tells us he loves us.

What have you learned about yourself?
I have learned that I can parent and have noticed this evolving over time. Like any skill, you have to practise and you get better at it. You are often forced to react to something new and deal with it so you are constantly challenged.

I found it quite tough in the first year as we knew so little about each other but once we passed the first anniversary, this seemed like a milestone and things were better after that. After three years, I can parent with greater confidence and family life is more rewarding as a result.

Have you had to deal with attachment issues?
Like any adopted child, Scott has attachment issues. Early on, the slightest thing would affect him deeply. He would be quick to fly off the handle and get over-excited or very angry and it was difficult to get him back to normal. I went online and looked at parenting forums and devised a strategy to help him. He used to scream before leaving for school but now I know better how to manage his behaviour and emotions. We know the likely flashpoints and are much calmer. It is important for him not to feel abandoned, so if he has to have time out we sit with him. We also try to encourage eye contact and have some exercises to help with this. When he was younger, he would sit on our laps facing us and we would feed him and let him grab our noses – this encouraged him to look at our faces and give eye contact.

Part of our strategy is being very clear about what is happening in the day and having rules. We have a noticeboard in the kitchen with family rules like: put shoes on quickly when asked, no screaming, no hitting and be nice to each other. Children respond well to rules.

We had some attachment therapy, organised through Social Services, which was a great help. It would be useful to be able to call an expert sometimes to get advice – it would be good if post-adoption support was clearer.

Scott relies on us more and more as a source of consolation, whereas at first he would run away when he was hurt. It was really nice when he first sought us for solace. Now he asks to snuggle up, whereas before he used to put his knees or something else between us.

Apparently, seven is a crucial age in terms of attachment so we may need more help, but I think Scott is going to be OK as he has shown he can build meaningful relationships.

Have your friends and family been supportive?
Our parents and wider family and friends have been supportive and I hadn't realised how vitally important this would be. It is far better to have family and friends helping rather than some random babysitter. We hadn't expected some of our gay friends would volunteer to babysit but they have been great. Our neighbours, who are gay, also babysit and understand that we need a break sometimes. You need all the help you can get. We also have a childminder, who is in her fifties. She is very flexible and helps out before and after school if we can't get home. It would be hard to do our jobs without her.

Have you experienced any homophobia?
I haven't experienced any as a gay parent and I have been featured in newspapers and on television, telling our story. I wrote an article for a national newspaper and there were some negative comments online but they were far outweighed by the positive ones. On the whole, I have been struck by how supportive everyone has been.

When you are walking down the street, people don't necessarily know you are a gay parent, but in any case, I feel totally relaxed.

What impact has adoption had on your finances?

Luckily, we are well paid but we also budget carefully and plan our expenditure. Children's clothes can cost a lot but we have learned not to spend too much on them as Scott is constantly growing out of them.

And on your work?

It changes your attitude. You have a different set of priorities and your life outside of work is more important. My work used to be unpredictable and involve long hours so sometimes it could be difficult if I came home exhausted and had to start childcare immediately.

I was made redundant at the beginning of this year and that allowed me more time to do childcare. The flexibility of not working was great but I now have another job, which has more regular hours.

And on your relationship?

Having a child can be stressful and you have less time and energy for each other. It can amplify any difficulties, so you need to have a strong relationship to start with. You also need to try to have date nights and enjoy the time you have together in the evenings. My advice is to share responsibility as much as possible and think about each other's feelings, make sure there isn't any resentment building up.

Have you discussed your sexuality with Scott?

We have always made it clear to him that there are different types of families and there are others like him in a similar set-up. We don't want to make a massive issue of it and so far he seems to be taking it in his stride.

How do you feel about not being a birth parent?

I don't know what it's like to be a birth parent. From what I understand, there is often an instant surge of feeling when a child is born. With us, we were delighted when we first saw Scott but our love has grown and right now is stronger than ever. I think sometimes not being genetically related means you have less preconceptions about how they should behave or what they should achieve.

What advice would you give about managing routines, boundaries, rewards, sanctions, television, computer time, etc?

These are all very important and saying no has to mean no. You have to be robust but pick your battles and don't escalate things. Be very consistent with your boundaries. In terms of television and computer time, we don't have strict rules but if they have been on too long, we turn them off. Sometimes Scott can be a bit upset by this. Children can get sucked in to computer games and become distressed when they have to come back to reality, so it is important to monitor how long they spend on them.

How have you explained Scott's past to him?

We made a slide show on the computer that tells the story of his life. We found a template and did it ourselves as the social worker wasn't helping us to do it. We managed to find a photo of his first house and have a photo of his mother and his foster carers. We have shown this to him regularly. It is important to go back to it as his understanding increases. For example, he hadn't registered initially that he had a birth father.

What has been your experience of holidays?

We travel a lot and this has been a good bonding experience. To start with Scott was quite nervous but now three years on, he gets excited and we can look forward to it and this helps with our bonding. Justin's parents live in North America so he takes him there for four weeks in the summer holidays and usually I join them for at least two weeks. They go fishing, stay in cabins, make bonfires – all of this fills Scott with excitement. It gives us a sense of being a family. Scott likes the outdoors, going on adventures, skiing, camping, the seaside – we haven't had any bad experiences.

What have been some of your successes with regards to pursuing hobbies/activities together?

Scott loves water, so swimming has been a big part of our bonding. It allows us skin contact, especially in the early stages when he would cling to me and rely on me more. This has been good for developing an attachment.

What has been your experience in terms of showing physical affection to Scott?

Now he really wants to snuggle up. It is important not to be forceful and to respect his space. I feel quite relaxed around him and it is important to be as natural as possible, while being sensitive to his needs and past experiences.

What advice would you like to give to prospective adopters?

We talked about it so much and were often in two minds about it, but seeing other people doing it helped us – I would really recommend New Family Social as you can join it and go to events even before you have children placed with you.

We thought there would be a lot of intrusion from social workers and that we were opening ourselves up to risk and uncertainty, but it has been worth it.

It's a massive upheaval but three years on, it just seems like a normal part of our life – I would say get support, read books, meet other people who have done it and if you are ready, go for it. Gay people have always been part of family life – they are brought up by families, so why shouldn't they have families of their own?

6 Stephanie and Jenny

Stephanie, 41, a play therapist and Jenny, 35, who works in the finance industry, fostered Neil when he was eight years old. He is now 14. They are in the process of applying for a special guardianship order (SGO). This is a court order that became available under the Adoption and Children Act 2002. An SGO gives the special guardian legal parental responsibility for a child until they are 18. The child is no longer the responsibility of the local authority and although birth parents retain their legal responsibility, the special guardian only has to consult them in exceptional circumstances.

Stephanie tells their story.

Why did you decide to foster?

We both wanted to look after children. Out of the two of us, I was the more maternal and always wanted children to be a part of my life. I had already been working for seven years in a centre providing therapy for children with attachment disorders. My passion was to work with children with challenging behaviour to try to understand what was behind this. Usually, they have very traumatic backgrounds and many have been through several foster homes. Jenny was particularly interested in supporting children with disabilities.

We started off doing respite fostering. Neil came to us during this time, when his foster care placement broke down. It was a temporary measure until they found a longer-term placement. When he moved to his new foster home, we maintained contact through visits and letters.

We then decided to try to have a baby through donor insemination. I became pregnant but lost the baby at 23 weeks. Obviously, I had to go through a healing process after this very sad loss.

About a year after Neil had moved to his new foster home, the social worker called us to say that Neil's relationship with the foster carer was breaking down and to ask if he could come and live with us again. We took some time to consider it as we didn't want to rush into a decision but it felt right and we have never looked back.

Neil has needed support through the child and adolescent mental health service (CAMHS) but he is growing to be a very confident young person. He is very much part of our family, for example, he sees my mother as his Nan.

For the last two years, we have also been offering respite foster care for a nine-year-old boy with Down's Syndrome. He comes to stay for the weekend, once a fortnight. That's been fantastic and a very different experience for me.

We have also recently started fostering a nine-year-old girl, Katie. Her mother has mental health issues so we are not sure how long she will stay with us.

How has fostering affected your work?

A few years ago, I took redundancy from work and retrained as a play therapist, so I now only work two days a week. It is quite difficult balancing all the children's needs and finding time for meetings with social workers. On top of this, Jenny's father died recently so she has gone out to Dubai to be with her mother. She needs to be out there for quite a while, maybe a year.

How are you managing on your own?

I am just getting on with it but it is physically demanding, doing all the cooking, cleaning and ironing. Luckily, my brothers and sisters live nearby, so they help out. Thank God for Skype – Jenny and I talk for ten minutes a day.

The key is to make a bit of time for yourself even if it means going to the cinema in the middle of the day or going to the gym for an hour.

Have you had any respite?

I am going out to Dubai for two weeks to join Jenny. Neil is going to stay with my mother for a week and the other week he'll be at Scout camp. Katie is going to stay with her grandmother.

How much support have you had from the local authority?

We have had the same link worker since we started fostering, which is very unusual but great for building up a relationship. We have also had amazing support from the two CAMHS (Child and Adolescent Mental Health Services) workers. There are two family therapists within the local authority whom we can also call on to discuss issues.

How would you describe your experience overall?

It is extremely rewarding to see a child change from the time when they arrive at your door with a small bag of things to becoming a confident and mature young person, contributing to society and pursuing activities with a circle of friends.

I think we have made a difference by offering a secure base for a child who has never had one. However, you also have to be prepared for it all to be chucked back in your face, when they become a teenager and say, 'You can't say that, you're not my mum'. This can be hurtful but all children can do that, even to their birth parents.

What was it like in the initial stages when Neil moved in?

It was quite difficult because his moods and behaviour changed before and after contact with his mother. His relationship with his mother was very fraught. Now his mother has matured and Neil is growing up, it is better. They now have contact, supervised by a social worker, every couple of weeks and he also sees his father every few weeks, unsupervised – they go shopping or have breakfast together. We consider that we share the role of parenting with his mother and father. In effect, he has three mothers and a father. This level of contact will remain, even if we get the SGO.

Neil has had therapy to make sense of his early years. He struggles with being different and having social workers in his life. He just wants to be like everyone else. So that is why we are keen to get the SGO. We applied for the SGO with continued financial support until he is 16. Once that comes through he will no longer be in foster care and we won't have to have six-monthly Looked After Child (LAC) reviews, which he hates.

At the moment, we have to ask Social Services if he can play a PlayStation game that is above his age group when his friends are playing games suitable for 16-year-olds. We talk to him about the suitability of games, especially if they are violent, but it would be easier if we could make the decision ourselves. Once you have had a few years' experience, I think you should be able to make more decisions.

What difference has it made being a lesbian foster carer?

I don't think it has made any difference. We have been very fortunate and not experienced any homophobia. The social workers were very positive about us even though they didn't have any other same-sex couples on their books. I sometimes wish there were other same-sex couples on our training sessions. However, all the people we have met have been very welcoming.

We have also been very lucky with Neil's friends and their parents. As teenagers, most of his friends think it is quite cool to have gay parents, for example, calling us by our first names. Some new neighbours moved in when Neil was younger and he just introduced us as his two mums and the man next door was totally cool about it. I think society is changing for the better.

It has been interesting seeing my mother change over the course of me coming out and fostering children. She has changed her views and become very positive. We gave respite care to two boys for a while until they were placed for adoption with two gay men. When I told my mother, she just said, 'So they are going to have two dads, what do they do?'

What have you learned about yourself?

I have had to look at my styles of parenting. Normally, I am very patient and nurturing but when things get hard I have very strong boundaries. I believe young children need boundaries and routines alongside nurturing. However, Jenny sometimes says I've been a bit hard, so I look at my parenting and sometimes see that it stems from the way I was parented. We are all shaped by our own experiences of childhood.

Recently, Katie has been ill before and after contact. I'm not so patient with illness and I think that stems from my childhood. My mother wasn't so patient when we were ill.

What difference do you think it has made not being a birth parent?

My experience of losing a child was very big for me and part of me wishes I could have had a birth child. I have always had a good relationship with children and see myself as a bit of a universal mother. It is hard to know if it would be different, it is a difficult question. I think I love Neil as much as I would a birth child, it is a genuine love that has grown over our five years together and I know he will be part of our lives forever.

I also love the role of fostering and feel very fortunate to be able to do it. You can feel the love growing for the children you foster. I popped my head into Katie's room the other night to check on her and thought what a lovely, sweet girl.

What impact has fostering had on your lifestyle?

It was a big transition. We were used to city breaks, going up to London and having fancy holidays but I think I have adapted naturally to mothering. I had many years of nights out, going to festivals and I think I grew out of them.

Parenting is a full-time job but you still need to take time out for yourself as it takes its toll emotionally and physically. Now I enjoy going for walks or doing charity runs. My peer group has also changed – most of them have children and we go round to each other's houses rather than to the pub.

And on your relationship?

It has been very positive – when you first get together you are wrapped up in each other but it is nice to see each other grow into the role of parents. When we first fostered Neil I was putting all my energy into making sure he had the best of everything but you need to find a balance. It can be so exciting to be parenting but you need to make sure it doesn't consume your whole life.

There is a seven-year age gap between myself and Jenny. She always knew I wanted children from the start of our relationship. It is lovely to see her growing naturally into a mother. I think we complement each other. She can be softer and we have discussions about how to meet in the middle. It is a learning experience for both of us.

How do you share responsibilities?

When we first fostered Neil, we were both working full-time so we had to share responsibilities. We played to our strengths, for example, Jenny used to be a chef, so she would do more of the cooking and I managed the administration of fostering as I used to do that as part of my job.

How have you explained your sexuality to the children?

When we were going through the assessment process, we worried about how we were going to talk about it, but in the end we decided not to make a big fuss of it. Neil quickly accepted it and as he grew up he asked more questions, which is very natural. We didn't keep anything a secret.

What was it like when Katie moved in?

When Katie first moved in, she was very demanding and always wanted to be the centre of attention. She was very traumatised about being taken from her mother and this made her very clingy. She always wanted to know where I was. It took time to reassure her – one of her first questions was 'Are you a safe adult?'. That is a huge thing for a nine-year-old to have to ask and I could only prove to her over time that I was reliable and consistent. It was a very emotional time as you feel the stuff that they bring.

It was also demanding, managing the big change for Neil. He was testing me to see if I would still be there for him, so it was a very tiring time.

How have you managed some of the emotional and behavioural issues the children have displayed?

Neil had difficulty managing his feelings, particularly his anger. He would have very angry outbursts and we used to have to hold him to calm him down. It can be quite traumatic. He was testing to see if we were strong enough physically and emotionally. Some incidents would last several hours, which was very tiring all round.

He had therapy to help him manage his feelings. He had a lot of stuff stored up and it was about peeling back the layers. It was also about learning that he could trust us.

Neil can now calm himself – he recognises signs in his body and knows that he doesn't have to swear, kick and shout. He can punch a bean bag or go for a run around the park or do breathing exercises. It is amazing to see the difference in him.

We have also had support from the family therapist and read books about anger and loss, particularly by Margot Sunderland, which are very practical. There is also a good book for children, called *A Volcano in my Tummy*.

It is very important to read about attachment disorder as elements of it will be relevant to all children in care. There are good books, research and training courses to help you. There is always hope that you can repair the damage done in the early years and you should use your supervisor to help you through this.

When Neil was living with his birth family, there wasn't much food in the house and for some reason he could never tell us he was hungry. We gave him a cake tin, which always had something in it, so that he didn't have to ask for food. That worked well for him and now he easily says when he's hungry.

How have you dealt with sibling rivalry?

Neil was so used to being number one that we had to talk to him seriously about fostering another child. He was excited about it and we prepared him well for it. However, Katie is very intelligent and can be manipulative. When we were trying to help her settle in, Neil was put out about it. He told my mother that Katie always wanted hugs. At least he was able to talk about it.

Over time, things have become more normal again for him and it has been a positive experience for them both – they get on well despite some niggles. It has been good for Neil to learn to share. We have managed to reassure him that there is still enough love for him.

How have you explained the children's pasts to them?

Neil has always been very willing to talk about his past. We have sometimes had to remind him when it was appropriate to talk about things as he went through a phase of spilling out everything everywhere. It is fine with us and some friends, but he needed to learn when it was appropriate.

It is important to go at the child's pace and not to probe or push them. Katie is very closed but I have always said to her that if she wants to talk about anything, I'm here.

How have you handled any issues around the children's sexuality?

Neil has questioned who he is as a natural part of growing up. The messages we give him are that it's about who you meet and who you decide to love. We have given him literature about puberty and he talks to my oldest brother, who is a real man's man. They have what they call "man-chats".

What has been your experience of the teenage years?

Neil can be moody but I feel quite confident about dealing with the teenage years as I have worked with lots of young people. It is a big transition with all sorts of changes in their brains. You just have to be patient and think of it like going through the terrible twos.

What would you recommend in terms of setting and managing boundaries, rewards, sanctions and routines?

For most children in care, routine is vital, especially in the early stages. Sometimes I think it sounds quite anal but structure is very important. It is about helping them to trust that things will happen on time and it helps them to settle. Boundaries are very important for all children.

In terms of routines, you have to be careful if children are used to something from their birth or foster family. For example, Katie wanted to watch every soap opera under the sun. I thought they were very depressing for a nine-year-old, especially just before bedtime. I talked to the social worker about it and we decided to tread carefully, as this was what she was used to doing with her mother. I let her watch *Coronation Street* and then introduced her to games like Uno to give her other options. You have to do it gently.

I don't like the term rewards. I think it works for some children but I prefer to use praise, which I think is vital. However, it needs to be natural, don't overdo it. We will reward Neil sometimes, for example, giving him extra pocket money for getting a certificate at school.

You need to have positive and negative consequences to behaviour but I like to get to the bottom of the bad behaviour before dishing out the consequences. An example of a sanction could be grounding Neil for an evening.

What has been your experience of holidays?

We have had some good experiences but some have been a nightmare. It can unsettle children and you don't know what their experiences might have been before. You need to be emotionally attuned to them. We have had some fantastic experiences like taking Neil on a plane for the first time and to a campsite in Wales.

My advice would be to make sure there is stuff they can do independently and if possible take a friend.

What have been some of your successes with regards to pursuing hobbies/activities together?

Jenny has been successful at getting Neil into Lego building – she used to do that with her dad. We have also got him into cycling, walking and Scouts. It's about finding out what they like and showing an interest in it as well as showing them things that you enjoy. I'm not into the Playstation, so he has to do that by himself.

What has been your experience in terms of showing physical affection to the children and their response?

I think with a child placed long-term, touch is vital for their healthy development. It is about being natural. However, I've never forced my affection onto a child and have always tried to go at their pace. You can't turn a child away who wants a cuddle or their head stroked when they are poorly.

How do you feel about safer caring policies?

I struggle with safer caring policies. If I was tickling my nephew, how can I not tickle my foster son? Sometimes I think the policies are not realistic and the needs of the children should come first.

Have you ever had any respite care and how did you handle this?

We went to Vietnam for our anniversary and Neil went to another foster carer, who he knows. I wouldn't want him to go to a stranger. Even so, it is hard to prepare them for respite. Over the last six months, there is no way I could have put Katie into respite care. Emotionally, it would have been too much for both of us, we would have really struggled.

I am looking forward to my 12 days off when Neil is going to Scout camp and my mother's and Katie is going to her grandmother's. Neil is looking forward to it because he is settled and secure. There is a lot going on for Katie anyway but I have to remind her that it is coming up. I ask her questions about it so that she has an opportunity to express her feelings. We have started to pack a few things in preparation. Part of it is also reassuring them that you will miss them.

What would you say to people thinking of fostering?

Think about what suits you – whether it's respite fostering, short-term or long-term. Make sure you have a good support network around you. In terms of finances, independent fostering agencies pay a lot more. We do it for a local authority but I think they should pay more.

Overall, it's so rewarding and such a privilege, it is hard to put it into words. With the social work team it is like being part of a big, extended family. There is a lot of support out there. I love what I do and that's simply it. If you are looking to have a family, there are lots of children out there who need a loving home.

Neil, aged 14

How long have you been in foster care?

I have been in care for eight years and it's not always been easy. When my sister and I first went into care, we were excited because we liked change and we wanted to know where we were going to live. It was not long before we were moved from our first placement and that felt sad for us. We were then placed in different homes, separately.

I don't like telling people I am in care. It can be hard if you are with a carer for a long time and then you are moved, it's sad to say goodbye.

I am very happy with Steph and Jenny. I love them. It was not always going to be long-term as it just started as respite. I moved away and then came back again.

I went through about six placements before settling with Steph and Jenny. My sister, who is older, now lives with her boyfriend in her own home. This saddens me. I am now going to have special guardianship and my sister wishes she had this.

How do you feel about your birth parents?

Sometimes, I miss my mum and dad. I know they couldn't look after me but I see my dad and can arrange it without supervision. With my mum it's different because of her boyfriend, so contact has to be supervised. We normally go to the cinema. Overall, I enjoy it more with my dad because I also get to see my little sister. It's nice to catch up with them.

What has it been like growing up in this family?
It's been good. I've enjoyed living with Steph and Jenny. It is a nicer house and nicer environment than if I'd stayed with my parents. You get pocket money and more opportunities. If I lived with parents, I wouldn't be as good at Maths and English.

Have there been any issues for you growing up in a same-sex family?
They aren't any different from other carers. If friends come round to the house, I tell them they are lesbians. Some people are stupid and ask questions like, 'Do you hear them at night?' so I just ask if they hear their parents at night.

When I came to live with Steph and Jenny, I was only young and didn't think about them being lesbian and wasn't really bothered about it.

Sometimes there are only women in the house and that can be a bit annoying. It would be nice to have a man in the house sometimes whom I could chat to, but I have men whom I can talk to, like my uncle.

What are your favourite activities?
I like going to the park, playing football, playing on my ipod and PlayStation, Scouts, swimming and my drama group.

I also belong to Voice, a club for foster kids. We talk about what it's like being in care, what could be improved, what we are going to do when we leave care.

What is it like having a foster sister?
It is alright but a bit irritating sometimes. I like having another kid in the house for the company – adults can be a bit boring sometimes. In some ways it was better on my own as it was less complicated and Steph had more time, but also now it means she is not always focused on me.

What do you want to do in the future?

I want to go to college, study engineering and get a good job. I also want to have kids when I'm older but I'd prefer to adopt or foster – I'd rather make a difference.

What would you say to gay men and lesbians thinking of becoming foster carers?

Don't be ashamed to say you are lesbian or gay, just say this is who we are and we're going to be looking after you.

Katie drew this picture.

7   Cliff

Cliff, 34, a single, black teacher, adopted a five-year-old boy, Marcus, three years ago and has recently adopted a four-year-old boy, Henry. Both children are dual heritage. They all live together in London.

Cliff tells his story.

Why did you decide to adopt?

I have three brothers, two of whom were adopted by my mum and dad. I had always wanted to adopt children myself and thought I would do it after having my own children. That was before I realised I was gay. I was asked by a good female friend to have a child with her and I went to counselling with her and had medical tests, but in the end I dropped out as I wanted to be a full-time father. Having a baby with a woman would have meant not having sole responsibility.

How did the adoption application process go?

I went through my local authority. The process went quite smoothly. I had an initial conversation with them that was positive, so I then took the first step of moving into a larger flat, as previously I was living in a one-bedroom flat.

I was the only single, gay person on the preparation training course. There were a few gay couples and lesbians in the group. In fact, I was the first to be matched successfully with a child. However, to achieve this I had to be very proactive – I was on the social worker's case all the time. They have so much going on that I think you have to push otherwise you are sidelined.

During the home study, I made sure we had assessment meetings every couple of weeks. Otherwise, it would have taken much longer. You hear horror stories of how long it can take and I wonder why people let that happen. You have to go to the top to complain, if necessary.

The second time around, six local authorities refused to consider me because I only had a two-bedroom flat, even though I was proposing to move into the smaller bedroom and let the boys share the larger one with bunk beds. I don't think the rejection was based on homophobia or discrimination but I did feel let down by the original local authority that had approved me the first time.

Luckily, one local authority said it wasn't a problem and I have now moved into the smaller bedroom and the boys are happily sharing – I grew up like that and I think it is good for children to learn to share.

How did the matching process go?

After the first approval everything went quiet for a while. I found Marcus' profile through the magazine *Be My Parent* and called up about him and gave my social worker's details. I got a phone call from my social worker who wasn't too pleased as I was doing her job for her. It felt like a good match as Marcus was born in the same town as me in the Midlands.

As Marcus is "mixed race", when it came to finding a match the second time around I wanted to find a child who looked like him so that they could pass as brothers. The social worker approached me through the family finder service. I was sent a poor quality video and one photograph. I thought, he's the right age, "mixed race", no disabilities – I knew I wouldn't be able to take on a child with disabilities because of being single and working. So there was no reason to say no. However, it makes me cringe, searching for children. It's horrible having to choose.

The second time around, once I was approved, the matching was fast-tracked because I had adopted before.

What would you say to someone thinking of adopting as a single person?

From my experience, you have to make sure you have a good support network. If your family is on board that is even better. I have an amazing family – they play a vital part. I realise now how much I need them.

You have to expect the unexpected – I didn't think I would need to leave work early so many times in the first few months – it is not as simple as taking adoption leave and then going back to work. My first child found school difficult so I was often called and asked to collect him early. I used to pray my phone wouldn't ring while I was at work but when it does you have to go.

I'm on adoption leave now for my second child but I am due back at the start of the next academic year. I took six weeks' adoption leave and then had the summer holidays, so he will have had 12 weeks to settle before I return to work. I opted for school-age children because I couldn't have managed otherwise and I couldn't afford to take more time off work.

What are the children like?

Marcus and Henry both come from large families with siblings, who had all been taken into care before they were born. Marcus and Henry were taken into care very early and were therefore not so affected by their birth families. They were in stable foster families. They both have very strong personalities. When Henry moved in four months ago he quadrupled the noise level!

How do the children get on with each other?

They get on fine, playing together, arguing and fighting just like typical brothers. Henry has had a fantastic impact on Marcus – his behaviour has improved and he has been taken off report at school. I think part of it is getting rid of more energy at home and maybe he feels more responsible now as the older one.

What have you learned about yourself?

This has definitely been the right decision for me – it is the best thing I have done in my life. I'm probably happier now as a father than I have ever been, even though sometimes I am tearing my hair out.

What impact has adoption had on your lifestyle?

A year before I started the adoption process, I started cutting down on clubbing, etc, to make sure I could change my lifestyle and get used to it. Clubbing and going out was never satisfying enough for me anyway. I knew I wanted to do something more significant.

How have your friends and family been?

My main support is from my two very close friends – one male and one female, who both have grown-up children. They have given me such good advice. My younger brother, who is also adopted, has a very close relationship with the children and he helps out. My dad and stepmum come to help whenever they can. I have a large family and everyone plays their role.

The children really enjoy having grandparents, cousins, aunts and uncles – they didn't have that in the foster home. Henry does still talk about his foster mum and foster dad but he can't stop talking about his new grandpa and grandma.

How much contact do you have with the children's birth families?

We have letterbox contact for both of them. I write once a year but I have never had a response. We stay in touch with of one of Marcus' sisters, who is adopted, and they see each other and exchange presents. I have searched for the names of the older siblings and his mum on Facebook and seen photos of them. I haven't shared this with him yet as he is too young.

What is your greatest achievement?

I think it is seeing how they have done so well at school. Obviously, as a teacher, education is very important to me. Marcus, who was five when he came to live with me, didn't know his alphabet and couldn't count past 10. Nothing has made me prouder than to see his academic progress and how he's grown in confidence.

He recently won first prize in a talent competition for singing. He practises at home but wouldn't perform in front of anyone else for ages so it was a huge obstacle for him to get over. He also now sings in church.

Have there been any surprises?

The information you get from Social Services about children never matches up with how they are in reality. I should have asked for a report from Marcus' nursery as that would have been revealing. He was behaving well at home but not at school. The foster carers hadn't mentioned this but they had a different attitude to me – they felt that whatever was happening at school was the school's problem, whereas I put sanctions in place at home to ensure better behaviour at school.

What are some of the emotional and behavioural issues you have dealt with?

Henry can be very defiant. If I ask him to do something he will just sit down and say no and smile. If I send him to his room for time out, he will be quiet and wait until I come up, whereas, Marcus will make as much noise as possible.

With regards to sanctions, you have to make sure that they are fully aware of why sanctions are in place and talk to them about it, otherwise they won't know what is naughty or why they are in trouble.

Marcus loves watching TV so stopping him works as a sanction. However, Henry doesn't, so I have to find other things that work for him.

Can you describe some of the activities you do together?

I like to tire them out so we go to the park a lot and we also live next to a leisure centre. We do crafts – making things out of papier-mâché. I try to find things that are free as otherwise it can be very expensive, especially theme parks. We visit a museum every school holiday.

Over the summer, we are going on a foreign holiday. I try to put together a timetable for the holidays, so that they know what they are doing. However, it's important to have days when they have to get on with playing by themselves, otherwise you wear yourself out.

What impact has adoption had on your finances?

It has had a huge impact. You really have to think about it. I can't remember the last time I bought myself something. Marcus is growing so much, I have to keep buying new clothes and shoes. At least Henry can have some of his clothes when he's grown out of them.

I remember my dad going on about leaving lights on and water running and now I'm saying the same things myself.

And on your work?

The first school I worked at was not family-friendly. Hardly any of the staff had children. If Marcus had an inset day, I would have to phone in sick to make sure I would still get paid. You couldn't bring children into school if they had a day off. I'm now working in a Christian school and it is much more family-friendly. If Marcus has a day off, he can come in with me and he is allowed to sit in the back of the class or colleagues will help out. The headteacher brings his kids in and everyone has been very supportive of the new adoption. You have to think about the industry you are in and your employer's attitude.

Have you discussed your sexuality with the children?

I haven't discussed it with Henry as he is too young, but I have had age-appropriate discussions with Marcus. I have made sure he understands about differences in families. He came home from school using the word "batty man". He didn't understand that it was an insult to gay men so I used it to start a discussion. He knows that I'm not in a relationship but that I could have a relationship with a man or a woman. He has met a gay couple I know and as he gets older I will discuss it more with him.

Unfortunately, he will hear homophobic stuff at school but he understands that I will not tolerate him repeating anything in an offensive way.

Have you had a relationship since the children moved in?

No, I haven't had time.

What part does religion play in your life?

I only started going to church again when Marcus came to live with me. I went to church as a kid and enjoyed Sunday school – you learn so much. My childhood was so happy and good, I'm trying to re-enact the best parts for my children. Marcus goes to Sunday school and I run the youth club on a Friday for the older kids while he goes to one for younger kids. A lot of people know us from church and he has friends from Sunday school. I'll be introducing Henry to it once he has settled in. The church doesn't know about me being gay. I'm not ashamed of being gay and I'm not hiding it but I don't talk about it openly with people who aren't close to me.

How do you feel about not being a birth parent?

The love I have for the children is as strong as any birth parent. However, it is something that develops, whereas for a birth parent it is probably instant. I found that the love quickly develops during the introduction period and continues as the child comes to live with you.

Henry started off calling me Cliff, which seemed a bit strange but now he calls me Daddy Cliff and says I love you when I say it to him. I think he is copying what Marcus says so I'm not sure it was very natural to start with but it is becoming more natural. Marcus calls me Dad, so I'm hoping Henry will just call me Dad when he's ready.

Have you talked about the children's pasts?

I've got a lot of information and they had extensive life story work with CAMHS – the child and adolescent mental health services – when they were aged three or four. I expect when they get older, more things will fall into place and they will want more detail each time.

I heard Marcus saying to a friend that he didn't have a mummy. I explained afterwards that he does have a mummy and that everyone has to have a mummy to be born.

Neither of them have ever asked about their birth families. Henry misses his foster family, particularly at night; he hugs his teddy and we talk about it. I have to be understanding about it. I explain that they were a fostering family until a forever family came along.

We are going on a plane for the first time together this summer and Henry asked if it will fly over his foster family's house and can we wave?

What advice would you give about holidays?

I think they are a fantastic bonding experience. A month after Marcus moved in we went to Spain and stayed in a hotel with a cousin. We had so much fun and excitement every single day. We were in and out of the pool. We are doing it again this summer and I think it will be a great experience for us all. However, in both cases, the local authority questioned it, saying it might be too early to go away.

What advice would you give to prospective adopters?

Find out about as much as possible in advance, especially your adoption leave at work. Think about building your support network from your family and friends. Work out your finances to see if you can manage.

Once you have been approved, ask as many questions as possible when a potential match is suggested but be prepared that you won't find out everything. I was told Henry was allergic to chocolate but this wasn't a medical diagnosis, it was just what the foster family believed. I wanted to test this out so I gave him some chocolate and he said he would go "loopy" but he didn't.

Luckily, children are adaptable. Marcus moved from an isolated farm to an inner city flat with no garden but he has adapted. Other people might have felt they couldn't offer him enough but I think I offer him other things.

I would recommend reading as much as you can about adoption. There is interesting research on the internet about adoption, most of it is American.

What other messages would you like to give?

Social workers need to have lower case loads. They make terrible mistakes. For example, I needed a passport for Marcus but when it arrived, it had his name on it but another child's photograph. Sadly, this didn't surprise me.

I think the adoption process should be speeded up. It took six months the second time around and that was being fast-tracked.

I also think that children who are adopted should continue to be in a high priority group for choice of schools. This will be better for the children and parents.

8

Andrew and Rick

Andrew, 46, and his partner, Rick, 48, have fostered two teenage boys, Jake, now aged 16, who has lived with them for three years and Jason, now aged 13, who moved in nine months ago. Andrew works in the care sector and Rick is an IT manager. They live together in the Midlands. They are all white British.

Andrew tells their story.

Why did you decide to foster?

We had been thinking about it for a long time. I have a lot of experience of working in the care system, particularly with foster carers and managing residential care homes. I was very interested in the impact of the care system on children. When I was working with a couple of foster carers, it made me think, Rick and I could do this. Rick is able to work from home, so we thought we could make it work.

How did the application process go?

The local authority did a recruitment drive but we weren't that impressed. We looked at three or four fostering agencies and went ahead with one of them. They did the first assessment within a month and were very efficient. One of the others rang a month after our initial enquiry. Fostering agencies should realise that you are probably going to ring quite a few agencies and that it is such a big decision to make that phone call, they should respond immediately. I think the response you get at this stage might reflect the support you are likely to get later on.

I was always up-front about the fact that I had managed fostering services. I didn't want people to think I would be hard to assess. It all went quite smoothly and we were approved for two boys aged 0-18 and have fostered two teenage boys.

What was it like when the boys moved in?

They had a long history of being in the care system and had had some poor experiences. When Jake moved in, it was just before he was about to start at a school which was a few miles away and we live in a rural area, so you couldn't rely on buses. We got a bit wound up about working out who was going to do the school run in terms of showing that he had two male carers. He said he wasn't bothered and I realised it was more my issue than his.

By chance, I had worked with Jason's previous foster carers. It was a good placement but they were due to retire, so his coming to us was a planned placement. We spent time bringing stuff to his room and we put a chart on the wall mapping out what was going to happen each day. As Jake had been here for two-and-a-half years already, we wanted him to be involved. He came to the planning meeting and asked all the questions adults probably wouldn't ask, such as what music does he like, what time does he get up and what happens if he gets into trouble at school.

In the first month, both boys were trying to find out how far they could push each other. Now it has settled down and their behaviour is just what you would expect of two boys – who is in control of the TV or laptop and every morning, they race each other down the path to see who can get in the car first. Overall, they get on well.

They both have similar backgrounds in terms of abuse and neglect but Jake will only tell a few people he is in care, whereas Jason will openly say he is in care. Jake has been in care since the age of four. He has four brothers in care, two in the same placement.

What are some of the challenges you have faced?
They have tested out how far they can push us away. They have told lies and tried to cover things up. They have also needed to try to be in control. It is not surprising given their background of not knowing when they are going to be fed, whether they will have to nick food, and worrying if mum is going to come home. In the past, they have had to be in control as the adults weren't in control. We are trying to teach them appropriate behaviour, to let them know that we can help them and that they can unload if they want to.

At one point Jake was physically and verbally harmful to us. We didn't know what was going on. It turned out that he thought if he could show how bad he was, his mum wouldn't want him back. It is easy to focus on the actual behaviour and not what is behind it.

Rick and I are like concrete blocks, we remain solid and consistent for the boys. We have had to be very clear about rules, for example, everything is switched off by 10pm. We have to show that it is possible to exist within rules. We also have to respond quickly to situations. We try to show them that they can choose their behaviour.

We haven't had any problem with drugs and alcohol. I think it is partly because they have seen the impact of addiction on people in their lives. Jake is quite clear that he doesn't want to start drinking or smoking. Recently, however, one of the girls in his group of friends got drunk. Jake rang the girl's mother and asked her to pick her up. She was very grateful to him.

We find birth family contact can be very difficult for Jake. It can take six weeks to build him up beforehand and six weeks after to get him back on track. His mother can be very harmful.

It is a very intense household. Jake is growing up really fast and has hormones pumping around.

What do you think are your achievements so far?

People who don't see them every day tell us they can see a dramatic change in the boys – they notice that they look happier and obviously feel safe. Sometimes, on a day-to-day basis it is easy to forget the difference you have made. It is also nice to get comments from their school about how well they have settled, especially when we look back at how difficult it was to make them think that school would be safe – they had not had a good experience of school before.

We help them put their experiences in context. Sometimes, they will say the teacher was cross with them because they are in care and we say, no, it is because you didn't do your homework.

Have you experienced any homophobia?

It was a big surprise to both of us that we didn't get any resistance from the birth parents about them being placed with two men. Jake doesn't have contact very often with his mother but she has never made any comment about it. Jason's mother has a history of being difficult but again there have been no negative comments. Our address is kept confidential because of other risk factors.

In terms of the wider community, we have lived here since 1995 and know people in the area. They have accepted us as a gay couple who are able to bring up two boys. However, we didn't know some of the parents who lived on the estate nearby. The boys play with other kids locally and quite rightly the parents have rung to check us out before letting their children come round to our house. One set of parents refused to let them come.

Jason and Jake have a wide range of friends and they all know that we foster them and live as a couple. I think it has been good for them to experience something out of the norm.

Sometimes, if Jason comes in with a bleeding knee, Jake will say don't be such a poof. I tend to say, it's OK to say that here because we won't be upset by it but you don't know if some of your friends might be gay and they might be upset if you use that word.

Do you think it has made any difference being gay carers?

We have said to both children's social workers when they were considering us as a match that there are advantages as we are not in direct competition with the birth parents.

In the past, they have had heterosexual foster carers, who divided up tasks in quite traditional ways. In our case, Rick has given up his full-time job to become a full-time carer but we share tasks. It is good for them to see men tidying up, washing, cleaning and caring for them. So hopefully by living here, we are challenging some of the stereotypes they have encountered before.

Jake has had a couple of girlfriends and wanted to impress them by cooking from scratch, so he learned from Rick, who is a very good cook.

How have you discussed your sexuality with the boys?

Right from the beginning, we made a booklet about our lives showing where we live and the fact that we have chickens, dogs, etc. We showed photos of the whole house including our bedroom, saying this is where we sleep. We made it very clear that we wanted a young person to understand that we are in a long-term relationship. We had a couple of matches before Jason but the social worker said the young people didn't want to live with us.

How about discussing their sexuality?

Both boys have experience of inappropriate sexual behaviour so we have had to be clear with them about appropriate and acceptable behaviour.

What have you learned about yourself?

The whole of my career, I have been trying to make a difference. However, you can have the world's best therapist or social worker but they are not there every day. Being a foster carer has made me realise how important day-to-day activities are, such as getting children up in time and making sure their uniform is ironed, which can sometimes be taken for granted by professionals.

I realise that we can have a big impact on young people's lives and life chances by breaking the long chain of abuse by parents, grandparents, uncles and aunts.

The testing out period was tough. You realise how strong you are inside. It is like having a very quick experience of being a parent without the previous nine or 11 years to draw on. Overall, it has been a good, positive experience.

Have you found the fostering agency supportive?

We had a newly qualified supervising social worker, so it was hard for them to supervise us although we said we are here to learn as much as possible. Supervision can help you to see the bigger picture. Jake has had two changes of social worker.

What advice would you give to social workers?

Make sure you have a professional reason for asking any questions of applicants. There are a lot of LGBT people out there who could offer a very caring home. You need to make it easier for a single, gay person to ring up and make sure they get a good response.

And to friends?

If you agree to be part of a support network, make sure you know what that means. Quite often people don't realise the kind of support adopters or foster carers need. I think assessors should meet and explain the responsibilities to people in the support network beforehand.

Have your friends and family been supportive?

My mother worked in children's services for a long time. She was always saying we desperately need more foster carers. Both my parents are very supportive. They said from the beginning that any children placed with us are going to have a good life.

Rick's father died a few years ago but he had a good relationship with him. His mother already has eight grandchildren but she said the boys will also be her grandchildren. We acknowledged that was a nice response but that she needed to realise that they may not see it that way. The wider family has also been very pleased for us.

We have had to be sensitive about Mother's Day, as it is difficult for the boys. We take our mothers out on a different day to celebrate it.

What impact has fostering had on your lifestyle?

I didn't realise it would have an impact on every aspect of our life – from the time we eat to what we eat, what time we get up and being involved in schools. I've also had to change my job to one involving less travel. I had to take a £12,000 pay cut but it is worth it to see more of the boys. If we have to do things differently, in order to bring up the boys, then we will. For example, if I'm working from home, once the boys are back from school, the laptop and Blackberry are turned off.

What has been your experience of holidays?

Jake was adamant that he didn't want to go on holiday, but we managed to persuade him to go on an outdoor adventure course and he enjoyed it. Jason would love to go away but Jake isn't very keen. We could ask Rick's mother to come and stay here to look after Jake but we are not keen to go away without him.

What has been your experience of other activities?

They often want to start something but then change their minds after a week. We'd like them to join clubs but they need to show more commitment. They would have us buying the most expensive football boots and then quitting after a week. We say they can join the school clubs and then if they show commitment they can join a local club. They love playing on bikes and we have lots of open countryside around.

What has been your experience of showing physical affection and adhering to safer caring policies?

We have to match what they want. Jason finds any physical affection quite hard unless he hurts himself. If Jake wants something, he'll give you a big hug.

We always make sure the bathroom door is shut and have said that their bedroom is private and we won't come in unless they want us to.

We all make sure that we wear pyjamas and dressing gowns and even when it's hot we insist on wearing a T-shirt at the dinner table.

Have you had any respite care?

We haven't felt the need for it and we think the impact on them would be quite big. My mother helped look after them when Rick's father died.

How are you preparing them for leaving home?

Jake is 16 and will stay here until he is at least 18. We are not the sort of carers who say you have to leave on your 18th birthday. He wants to go to college and we want to encourage that. He has also put down roots here so we want to help him settle in the area if he wants to, maybe in a flat nearby. We are trying to help him learn about budgeting, relationships, jobs, etc.

What advice do you have for people thinking about fostering?

Do as much preparation as possible before children or young people move in. Read about attachment and what it's like for young people to be in care. Find out about local schools.

Don't expect too much back from children or young people. I think a lot of people expect children to be grateful.

If you are fostering as a couple, make sure you take care of each other. It's important that you talk to each other and support each other and take a joint approach to parenting.

I think it is important that you have a strong relationship, as children will try to work out the weak points as it helps them to feel in control.

Young people's needs are so high and they can have a big impact on you, your relationship and the wider community.

I think your core task is to help the children repair the damage of their past and prepare for the future.

You have to be prepared for your private life to be open to scrutiny. We have had a trail of CAMHS (Child and Adolescent Mental Health Services) workers, teachers and social workers in our lives and you have to be prepared to be open to all of them.

Don't underestimate the skills you have. You will probably have a lot to give and can offer a safe and caring home even if you haven't had children before.

9

Francesca and Sarah

Francesca, 44, who is from South America, and Sarah, 44, who is white British, adopted a girl aged three from South America, and five years later another three-year-old girl from the UK. Andrea and Sophia are now 15 and 10 respectively. Francesca is a psychologist and Sarah is a teacher. They live in the south of England.

Francesca tells their story with some additional comments from Sarah.

What would you say to someone thinking of adopting?

I would say the same thing as to someone wanting to have a baby, be prepared to be challenged emotionally. Your life will alter dramatically and you will find it very demanding.

What has been the best thing you have achieved?

We are both mums, which is brilliant – something that we very much wanted. We are very proud of our girls and are so lucky. We have an amazing relationship with both of them. It is very special to have a deep, real and intimate relationship with them.

What has been the greatest disappointment?

We don't see things in this way. We have had many difficult times and situations but we don't see them as disappointing, just difficult. We managed some better than others. The difficult times have all served a purpose or taught us something important for the future.

Have there been any surprises?

The most surprising thing has been the intensity of emotion at times, especially when you are being challenged by the children. When we moved back from South America a year after adopting Andrea, I had a very low patch.

Andrea strongly favoured me for the first year and wasn't bonding with Sarah. This caused a lot of tension in our relationship. It sparked an intensity of emotion and I worried that it would stay like that forever. I knew the theory of splitting but all I could see was three people suffering. Eventually, you think, what is the worst that can happen? After thinking that I could never choose between my partner and my child, I realised it was essential to get them to bond. One thing that worked well was Sarah taking Andrea swimming regularly – she had to hang on to her, so that helped to build a bond between them.

When the same thing happened with Sophia but in reverse – she favoured Sarah – we knew it would not be permanent and I didn't feel the rejection so intensely. However, it was tough, particularly when she would say, 'Go away, you smell'. She also didn't like my more tactile style. I would want to just give her a spontaneous hug but she found that hard. I learned to approach her gently, let her play with my finger and then gradually show her that it was OK to be more tactile.

What has worked well for you?

Creating a full and secure relationship and maintaining this. A lot of people said, don't expect the children to love you. I remember being cross about this assertion. Why wouldn't they love you? What would be the benefit of not expecting them to learn to love and relate? You need to have positive expectations for your children but be aware that they won't fulfil them straight away – it could take years but they need to learn to love.

Life is full of ups and downs and we have to keep developing our bonds. We have prioritised this over insisting on other behaviour such as eating with a knife and fork when they were younger or academic achievement. We believe that if you focus on building a strong relationship, on their attachment needs, while modelling positive behaviour, children will end up assimilating and later copying that behaviour.

We have allowed the girls to regress when they needed to. Our social worker kept saying, be careful they don't stay in a regressed state, but we disagreed. Sophia slept in our bed for the first year and every morning she would hide under Sarah's T-shirt and come out again like a baby. It is so key to their development, allowing them to regress like this, because they have missed out on being able to behave in certain ways at key stages in their lives.

When we adopted Sophia she was three. We gave her a baby's bottle and Andrea wanted one too, even though she was eight at the time. We thought, why not, but some people might question it. Even though Andrea is 15 now, sometimes she wants to sleep in our bed if she is going through a tough time. We see this as a sign of her being able to be in touch with feeling vulnerable and to accept comforting. This is what then enables her to also function independently when needed, for example, managing her daily school life, flying to a different country on her own, applying for a job, etc.

What hasn't worked so well?
We had a difficult time when we were in South America for the first year of Andrea's adoption. I wasn't able to be out as Sarah's partner and this had a huge impact. At least with Sophia, she came to us as two mums who were together.

What have you learned about yourself?

I am more of an anxious parent than I thought I would be. I tend to like closeness, which feels safer for me. This could be one of many explanations for how the children connected to us and the splitting. Andrea also seeks closeness, while Sophia found the closeness too much.

Andrea could be very impulsive and quick to take risks. I had to learn to let her take risks while also offering guidance.

Sarah adds: 'I learned to be more patient and accept that I am wrong sometimes. Andrea and I could get into power battles and sometimes I had to admit that I was in the wrong. It is about learning ways of admitting you are wrong without losing authority.'

How much contact do you have with the children's birth families?

We didn't realise at the time we adopted Andrea from an orphanage that her 12-year-old sister was also living there. However, we kept in touch with the orphanage and found out that her sister went back to her mother. We go to South America once a year to visit Andrea's family. She is one of nine siblings. She is very aware of her birth family and finds it hard going to visit but is always glad when we have done it. It brings up very complex feelings for her and seems to be harder the older she is getting. Young children tend to relate to other children through play and so can integrate more quickly. Now, as a teenager, do you talk or play? There is also an issue with speaking another language.

With Sophia, her mother died just before she came to live with us. I'm glad we knew before she died that she was OK with us adopting her. Sophia has a maternal grandmother living in the UK and an uncle living in America. Contact with her grandmother has become less formal over time. We used to accompany her at set times but now she can go out with her grandmother by herself. Her grandmother also comes to school concerts. Sophia is happy with this arrangement. We Skype her uncle in America and have met him twice.

Sophia had contact with her birth father once but he finds it hard to maintain contact. He came for one contact session and missed the next one. Social Services often suggest specific times for card/letter exchanges. We wanted to keep it loose, aware that her father may not manage a strict structure. This has worked well and Sophia is always pleased with the letters when they arrive. We have been open about the reality of his situation, explaining it in a way that helps Sophia understand her father's difficulties.

Sarah says: 'Initially, I feared rejection during contact but actually the children appreciate us being there. I no longer see contact as a threat. The most important thing is that they feel we are there with them and later can share the range of emotions and conflicting thoughts they experience. Putting time aside for processing and supporting them after the contact is crucial.'

What has been your experience of dealing with schools?

It is important to assume that schools won't necessarily understand much about adoption or lesbian and gay families in terms of the children's needs. You have to liaise with them and put it in a way that they understand. Go in with a clear list of things to discuss. For example, Sophia was very shy and wouldn't ask for help with anything at school. We wanted her to feel safe in school and to learn to talk to teachers about her needs. We gave a booklet to her teacher, which had faces representing feelings in it. We asked Sophia's teacher to check in with Sophia before lunch every day. Sophia would choose a face to show how she was feeling and if she was not feeling well, she would be asked if her mums needed to come and get her. The first time she said she wanted to come home, I went in and we had lunch together and actually she ended up staying. We weren't called in again!

It is helpful if parents and teachers assume children are anxious even if they don't show it. At times, they can be pretty terrified and appear perfectly fine but children can often act out later on, either in school or when they get home.

PSHE (Personal, social and health education) lessons can be difficult when they are talking about family, drugs, domestic violence and prison. Teachers need to understand that children can't ask to leave when a lesson is difficult because this would draw attention to themselves, so it is important to ask them privately before and give them a chance to have an excuse not to be there. In secondary school, it could be useful to give all children prior warning about issues to be discussed so they could plan for it. If parents also know in advance, they can support children at home. Parents will need to take the lead in liaising with schools to get the relevant information.

What advice would you give to friends and family?

Give new families lots of space and be supportive but not intrusive. Think of it like a family having a new baby, regardless of the age the child is when they are adopted. Check in with them and offer calm support, particularly at difficult times. Be mindful that the feelings may be intense and scary, so help parents put it all into perspective and offer appropriate help when needed. Don't escalate things by adding more frightening ideas or examples.

Relatives and friends also need to be aware that relationships develop in different ways. It's OK to not feel so familiar with a new child in the family and to struggle to connect. Keep investing and give it time.

Sarah adds: 'My parents were worried about what the children would be like given their start in life, but they met Andrea off the plane and it was love at first sight. They play an important role and show great interest in the children.'

What kind of post-adoption support have you had?

We haven't had very much but we are not great at asking for support, partly because we quite often see things differently from social workers. It is hard to go from relating to Social Services as your "assessors/judges"'to seeing them as a source of support. However, I wish we could have had someone who built a supportive relationship with us from the beginning and who could check in with us every now and again. A lot of what is needed as children grow older is simply support in normalising the different phases we go through as a family and considering whether any extra support is needed. A phone call once a year would go a long way towards keeping that line of communication open.

We have been to some workshops and have a strong lesbian and gay adopters' group locally, which has been incredibly useful.

Have you had to deal with any homophobia?
The worst homophobia was from my parents but they are lovely now. They are very strict Catholics so it was a big struggle for them. I wasn't really out to them and in fact we went through the first adoption without telling them. Once they knew, they were very supportive of our adoptions and very accepting of Sarah, but struggled to accept our relationship. They particularly struggled with us getting married but made a huge effort and came to the party. Things continue to improve. I don't feel angry with them about the past. They are doing their best.

It is interesting, important and encouraging to note that neither we nor the girls have faced any significant, overt homophobia from people around us where we live. Neighbours, school staff, friends, other parents, employers, social workers, health workers all seem fine about us as a same-sex couple with adopted children. Sometimes there is scaremongering that children adopted by same-sex couples will face additional problems because of homophobic bullying but that is not our experience. We do live in a particularly gay-friendly region and recognise that others may not be quite so lucky, but the positive cultural shift over the last few decades has been immense.

Have you had any practical help from other people?
We have had a cleaner at different times in our life. If you can afford it, I would recommend this so you can spend more time and energy on the children. We would have welcomed people helping out in practical ways in the early days, for example, bringing a meal around sometimes.

What impact has adoption had on your lifestyle? How have you adapted and what advice would you give?
Devote your life to parenting. It has to be the main thing you do. You need to have conversations beforehand about how it will change your life – you won't be able to go out nearly so much and there will be chaos and madness at first. It is like having a baby. People don't talk openly about how hard it is

and the fact that you don't necessarily feel love straight away or that there are many times when you just think you made a huge mistake or won't be able to manage. Just like many birth parents feel with a first baby. Luckily, as with first babies, nice things also happen that help you survive and continue to work on the difficulties. We managed because we had made a decision to do it but it would have been easier if everyone could have been more open about how hard it can be.

What impact has adoption had on your finances?

Now the children are in school we can carry on working, but I think it is very important for children to have one of the parents around. Long hours in day care is hard enough for birth children, and it can have a hugely negative impact on building relationships with an adopted child.

Sarah and I are lucky in that we can alternate being at home for them after school or going into school when needed. Even now that the children are older and spend much more time out, we still see the importance of working reduced hours so that one of us can be at home when needed.

What effect has adoption had on your work?

I would say it has enriched my work as a psychologist and I've learned a lot from the children. I have become even more passionate about children's welfare and parenting. On the other hand, keeping the focus on my own children and family has meant I have become less concerned about my career. As I've got older, I've realised I'm not hugely ambitious although I still enjoy my work.

Sarah adds: 'I applied for a deputy headship but didn't get it and am actually really glad. Since then I have consciously worked less hours, initially working part-time and eventually working full-time in a position that allows me more flexibility. It was a big shift in my career plan but I certainly don't regret it.'

What effect has adoption had on your own relationship?

The first year was horrendous. It was very stressful and then just as Sarah found her feet again, I became depressed. There were times when we questioned whether we should split up. If you can manage the tough times and work it out, it will strengthen your relationship. Now the children are 15 and 10, we have moved on a long way and through many ups and downs.

Adoption puts a lot of strain on your relationship simply because it presents you with lots of challenges and so can be very stressful. But like overcoming any challenge, it can also provide a positive way of growing your relationship. I admire Sarah's parenting and learn a lot from her. We talk about the children a lot and it has become part of the fabric of our relationship. We think very similarly about parenting, values and child development.

How have you managed if the children have played one parent off against the other? What advice would you give?

Be prepared for it. If you are strong in your relationship as a couple, it will still bother you and create tension and conflict, but you will be able to find a way of working together. Often it's not the children but something that is going on between you that they pick up on. You also have to accept that you may have different approaches and the children will work this out. We believe it's OK for parents to have different responses at times, as long as they are OK with this.

Have you discussed your sexuality with the children?

We are very open with the children. We kiss and cuddle in front of them and talk openly about issues such as homophobia. Sophia was asked at school to take in a photo of her parents' wedding and so she took one in of our civil partnership. Andrea has friends who are gay and is particularly aware of fighting bullying and prejudice.

What impact have racial differences had on your family?

This is a tricky one. I'm from South America but white-skinned, Andrea has darker skin and curly hair, Sophia is "mixed race" but paler than me and Sarah is white British, so we also have different cultures in our backgrounds.

We initially lived with Andrea in London, in a very ethnically mixed area. Andrea experienced a bit of "racist" bullying when we moved to a very white area on the south coast, where there were only a couple of "mixed race" children in the school. However, it was not very long-lasting and we talked it through together, focusing on people's difficulties in dealing with "difference".

Has religion played a part in your lives?

I was brought up Catholic. Sarah was always fairly sceptical of all institutionalised religions. The girls have been aware of different religions through discussions at school and at home. Andrea went through a phase of wanting to experience going to church and both Sarah and I supported her in that process, including going through first communion. She later changed her views but is still very interested in the more philosophical and spiritual side of various religions. Sophia is also going through a phase of being more interested in exploring religious concepts.

Have class differences had any impact on your relationship with the children and others in their lives?

We both come from very middle-class backgrounds while Andrea comes from a very poor background and poverty played a big part in her being placed in an orphanage. She is very aware of this difference and it brings up difficult feelings for her – she is acutely aware of what she has both financially and in terms of education and has mixed feelings about it. So far, Sophia seems oblivious to the differences or maybe it just isn't an issue for her.

How do you feel about not being a birth parent?

Sarah never wanted to be a birth parent whereas I always liked babies and was very curious about pregnancy but didn't need to have a birth child. I looked after many babies while growing up and when working in child protection. So perhaps I got to the point where I didn't have a huge need to adopt a little baby. Adopting a baby is also to some extent much more of a gamble as you don't yet know what the difficulties might be. We deliberately chose to adopt an older child rather than a baby.

Has adoption had any impact on your health?

I had terrible backache through the first few months with a stiff neck and pain down to my waist, but obviously I still wanted to pick up Andrea. I had similar back pain problems when adopting Sophia.

I was also quite depressed when we came back from South America after the first year. I felt I had to be the strong one while we were out there and then it hit me when we returned. Getting back to work and back to a routine eventually helped because I felt valued in other ways.

What emotional and behavioural issues have you dealt with?

When Andrea moved in she was very angry and aggressive. She would punch, hit and throw things. If I told her off, she would try to find Sarah and hit her, which matched the splitting that was going on. Keeping bad and good separate! When she was able to be aggressive towards me, I actually saw this as positive step, a sign that things were feeling less frightening and therefore she could take the risk to feel cross with me and feel good with Sarah.

To stop her hurting us, sometimes we would put her in her bedroom and wait outside but now we regret that. It is like saying she had to deal with this by herself. After we had Sophia and when Andrea was older, we did switch to using time out, where she had to sit near us for five minutes. You have to be more patient but in the long run it is more effective.

Andrea was also very clever emotionally and was good at getting us to make up afterwards by singing together. We always tried to see what her anger was about – it was nearly always about being scared of something.

One day when Andrea was aged about four, I picked her up from nursery and it had been raining heavily and was thundery. The nursery staff said the other children had been crying but that she was fine. However, she kicked the back of the car seat all the way home. At first I told her off but when we got home I changed my tone and said, come here a second. Responding to the change in the tone of my own voice, she let me pick her up and I said, there was a lot of rain and thunder and I wonder if you got scared and maybe you also then got cross that I wasn't there to protect you. She said, that's exactly what happened. Andrea is very receptive to that sort of approach. It is like bursting a bubble.

One time we were on a boat and everyone, except me, was jumping in and out of the boat to swim in the river. I was anxious about the cold but eventually went in for a quick swim. When I got back on the boat, Andrea was hyper and couldn't calm down. Eventually, I realised that because I had put a scuba mask on to swim she couldn't recognise me and didn't think there was anyone left to keep her safe. Although I knew she was safe and that I wasn't very far away or gone for very long, she didn't.

Sometimes, we say this behaviour isn't alright, so let's stop and see what's going on. You are offering them an alternative. I think you need to find ways to help them normalise their behaviour and feelings.

Have you had to deal with sibling rivalry?

Andrea was always very good at expressing her feelings, including conflicting ones. She really wanted a new sister and also worried about how she would feel about the new sister and whether she would have all the attention taken from her. Social Services nearly stopped the process because of Andrea verbalising her feelings. In fact, when Sophia arrived, Andrea was very protective of her and showed real empathy. One time when Sophia was crying, Andrea made a point of "explaining" to us that Sophia had lost everything, her toys, her bedroom, everything she knew.

Once Sophia had settled in and we were more relaxed, Andrea started expressing jealous feelings. At times she would say horrible things like she didn't want a three-year-old sister. We made it clear that certain things were not acceptable. She could say what she liked to us, but not to Sophia.

In some ways, sibling rivalry reinforces some positives, they can ask for our help to sort things out or we praise them if they sort things out for themselves.

They can at times compete a lot for our attention. We had to be very strict around bedtime routines and not let one child interfere with the other one's bedtime story, for example.

What advice would you give about managing routines, boundaries, rewards, sanctions?

We used to have a sticker chart for rewards, for doing things like making their beds, cleaning the guinea pig cage, playing well together, being helpful, expressing feelings and worries or doing homework. We also allowed Andrea to give some other stickers to Sophia so she felt a bit more empowered and included at the beginning.

When Andrea went to secondary school she started swearing and using the term "bitch'" We charged her 30p per swear word and said if she swore at Sophia, the 30p would go to Sophia. You have to find things that work without being too punitive.

We also take away computer time as a sanction. Andrea used to say it is not logical because it's not related to what she'd done wrong, but I believe parents sometimes need something easy that you can use without too much effort! A sanction also needs to be something that motivates them not to transgress again.

We will also sometimes use restrictions to motivate them to work on their relationship. For instance, we may say they can watch a film if they can agree on which one to watch – this makes them learn to negotiate.

Sophia used to sit at the table sometimes for an hour still eating her food. I would say, have you had enough and she would say no, I'm still eating. We didn't know what was going on. Eventually, I would have to take the plate away and say, you've had enough. We worked out that she simply couldn't say she didn't like something. At the age of five she decided to become a vegetarian because she had strong views about animal welfare.

How have you explained the children's pasts to them? Any advice or tips?

I believe in honesty. We have been very open and used age-appropriate language. We have brought it up and talked about it regularly rather than waiting for them to ask. Sometimes you can bring it up in relation to a film or book, for example, if a child has been abandoned, has to move or is showing relevant feelings in a story. We have noticed many story lines involve abandoned children or young animals.

How have you dealt with the children's anger?

Andrea would storm up and close the bedroom door. I would put a note under her door and she would engage with that and send notes back. It is about holding them and normalising their feelings. You can say things like 'I'm not surprised you are feeling this way'.

We always saw anger as linked to other feelings such as hurt and anxiety. So we try to work on what might cause hurt and anxiety. We have always done lots of soothing things, like putting little notes in their lunch box or giving them lip salves to take to school. We used these as transitional objects so that they would know we were thinking of them when they read the note or used the lip salve.

Andrea sometimes scratched herself and we would say, you don't have to do that and try to show her some other way to get rid of frustration. Sophia can also be obsessed with cleaning.

Have your children had any issues with drugs or alcohol?

This year, Andrea went to a party and later told us there was heavy drinking and even cocaine on offer. Andrea did not do any drugs and didn't drink very much but ended up having to look after friends. In a way I think it was a good experience for her as it scared her. She has a huge desire for independence and taking risks so it is about managing those risks. We have let her have some alcohol at home.

How have you handled any issues around the children's sexuality?

It's not easy. You have to deal with them talking about exploring sexuality at five and then later you have to decide on boundaries about having friends in their bedrooms, where they can go, with whom and at what time. It is hard to adjust to them growing up. Occasionally, I have objected to what Andrea wants to wear to go out or how she does her make-up but I am also willing to help her with make-up and choosing outfits. Sometimes, we simply bite our tongues and let her experiment.

Sophia went through a very "boyish" phase. She wanted to dress like boys and play like boys. She enjoyed the company of boy friends. Gender identity is a very complex issue and is developed slowly. Although Andrea was very keen to support Sophia's determination to challenge stereotypes, we were careful not to make it a bigger issue than it was and more our issue rather than Sophia's. So, as with her vegetarianism, we just supported the process and kept all possibilities open.

What has been your experience of their teenage years?

We are making sure Andrea feels a sense of belonging and are working hard to normalise difficult behaviours while still dealing with them. Sometimes she can feel ashamed of her anger and we have to share our own experiences, or those of people we know, to try to normalise it.

Have you experienced any homophobia from the children?

No, nothing at all. Sophia took longer to grasp the fact that we are gay whereas Andrea always seemed to be aware of it. Andrea couldn't understand why we couldn't get married – this was before the law changed. She wanted one of us to dress up as a man so we could get married. They have both grown up with us since the age of three so it is just part of life for them.

What has been your experience of holidays?

This has been very variable, sometimes fun and sometimes a nightmare. You have to keep in mind that it is likely to be stressful for the children. They might be anxious and out of their comfort zone as it is not familiar. We find they need to stand next to us more when they are uncomfortable.

It is also hard to predict when they are going to freak out about something. We went to a campsite and hired a cabin, with the girls sharing a room with bunk beds. Sophia was terrified about going to sleep, so in the end we had to open up a futon in the sitting room. I lay there with Sophia with the idea that we would spend the night chatting, telling stories. She eventually started to relax and fell asleep. Next day she slept in her own bunk bed without a problem!

I would advise looking ahead with the children, marking dates in the diaries and calendars to prepare them. Make booklets explaining what will happen with pictures of where you are going and how you are getting there. When you first arrive, explore the place with them before you unpack to help them to feel safe.

What have been some of your successes with regards to pursuing hobbies and activities together?

Andrea has always been very keen to try a variety of things but can get bored easily. Sophia struggles to join things and is shy at first but then finds it difficult to let go once she has joined something. We found a club for Andrea where you could try different activities such as archery, skateboarding, etc, and you pay by the month, so that suited her.

Sophia tried one activity at a time but once she got to the point of doing too much because she couldn't decide what to let go of. Eventually that became unmanageable and she had to make choices and stick to a few things she really enjoys.

They both enjoy horse riding and have learned an awful lot about themselves while working with the horses.

What has been your experience of showing physical affection to the children and their response?

Andrea has always been very demonstrative with her emotions, hence being quite aggressive when young. She will give and receive affection very comfortably and frequently, even when cross. She enjoyed rough play fighting when she was younger and big squeezes.

Sophia always liked more of a soft touch and prefers things to be more predictable. She didn't like it if I hugged her unexpectedly. You need to understand what children want and moderate your behaviour.

We had one phase with Sophia when she suddenly started hugging people, and it seemed a bit random and not so appropriate. I think when we were in South America she would hug people as she couldn't speak their language and she got a good response there. It became a good way of connecting with people, but she was not sure what to do next. We tried to see it as just a phase in the process of feeling more comfortable socially, so encouraged the niceness of the hug while gently moving her on once it became too much. It soon stopped being a problem and she became more chatty with people.

Have you ever had any respite care?
Nothing formal – the time we most needed it would have been the least appropriate and it wasn't worth jeopardising the relationship with the children. In the first year, Andrea slept at my sister's for one night. We were able to leave Sophia for an evening out a little bit earlier as she had her sister for company.

Sarah's parents look after them sometimes. They started doing it in our house and now they do it in their house and the children have stayed with them for a week.

How are you preparing the girls for leaving home?
We have talked about it along the way when they have asked questions, ranging from what would happen if we died to how to pay bills. We have also encouraged them to cook to prepare for the future.

Sophia was saying recently that she'd never leave home just as Andrea was beginning to think about taking a gap year before going to university. This definitely triggered anxiety in Sophia. Now that Sophia is moving to secondary school she is more able to talk about the anxieties around transitions while doing it anyway! So perhaps this has also made her more able to talk about her own future away from us… she will now talk about what she might do, where she might live, etc. But her questions are still about whether we would still be there for her such as, 'What if I have a pet rat in my house, would you come and visit?'

Is there any advice you would you like to give to social workers?

I think there should be more training around attachment issues for assessing social workers. They make far too many blanket statements about certain risks, especially in terms of inappropriate behaviours, without offering ways of working with such behaviours and normalising what they might be about. You risk parents and children being overwhelmed and creating shame and this is one of the worst feelings to deal with in life.

And to family and friends?

Be supportive and don't make quick judgments. Don't give the children negative labels; look at how to support the parents and don't criticise them or collude with the children.

And to schools?

Schools need to review their PSHE teaching and be more aware of adoptive families and mindful of how they are putting forward ideas. It would be better to divide the class into small groups so it is easier for children to explain things, if necessary. At primary school, they need to be aware of the implications of asking children to bring in a photo of themselves as a baby as some children may not have such photos. Give children choices such as asking for a photo of them at any time from being a baby upwards.

And to policy-makers?

Adoption leave should be the same as maternity leave.

Anything else to add?

When portraying different ways of having a family, adoption is always portrayed as one of the hardest; however, all the behaviours our children display could also be displayed by birth children. We need to be mindful of this and not just put their behaviour down to adoption. Of course their background will also play a part in their current difficulties. However, I sometimes worry that we get stuck with trying to use the past to explain all that is going on in the present and don't give enough attention to what might be going on right now. Present circumstances at school or at home, the way parents are interacting with each other and with the children, all play a huge role in how children deal with their present and past. If we want them to change the way they are dealing with life, are we prepared to do the same?

What resources would you recommend?

We are very lucky to have a local lesbian and gay adoption group. We just spent two nights with them at a youth hostel. The children enjoy spending time together and it is hugely valuable for us.

Children's books that we have found useful are:

Papa, Do You Love Me? (Mama) by Barbara M Joose and Barbara Lavallee (Chronicle Books, 2005)

Mama, Do You Love ME? by Barbara M. Joosse and Barbara Lavallee (Chronicle Books, 1998)

The Huge Bag of Worries by Virginia Ironside and Frank Rodgers (Hodder Children's Books, 2004)

Moving (Picture Puffin) by Michael Rosen and Sophy Williams (Puffin Books, 1995)

The books are not necessarily about adoption but help with emotions around loss, anxiety and moving home. Any books that help children deal with feelings are useful.

We find that many children's films are about children or young animals who lose their parents or suffer rejection, such as *The Lion King*, *Finding Nemo* and *Dumbo*. We always watch a film with them so that we can discuss it afterwards.

In terms of books for us, we have found the following useful:

What Every Parent Needs to Know: The incredible effects of love, nurture and play on your child's development by Margot Sunderland (Dorling Kindersley, 2007)

How to Talk So Kids Will Listen and Listen So Kids Will Talk (How to Help Your Child) by Adele Faber and Elaine Mazlish (Piccadilly Press Ltd, 2001)

Theraplay: Helping Parents and Children Build Better Relationships Through Attachment-Based Play by Phyllis B. Booth and Ann M. Jernberg (John Wiley & Sons, 2010)

Inside I'm Hurting: Practical Strategies for Supporting Children with Attachment Difficulties in Schools by Louise Bomber (Worth Publishing, 2007)

10 Lynn

Lynn, 55, white British, is a full-time carer who fosters teenage boys through an independent fostering agency. She started fostering when she lived with her partner. They had lived together for 17 years and had brought up her partner's two birth sons. She split up from her partner soon after they started fostering but Lynn decided to continue as a single carer.

Over the last six years, Lynn has fostered one young person for three years, who now lives independently, and two other 15-year-old boys. At one time she had three young people placed with her. Currently, Lynn has one 15-year-old boy living with her and is looking for another placement. They live in the South West of England.

Lynn was in care herself as a child and lived in 19 different homes.

Lynn tells her story.

Why did you decide to foster?

Being in care myself taught me a lot. It's frightening moving into someone else's house. I remember helping myself to a sandwich soon after I moved into one home and the next morning coming down to find notes on everything saying: 'Please don't help yourself'. This taught me what not to do.

When I was 28, I took six months to think about whether or not I wanted birth children. I decided against it and then my periods stopped completely.

It wasn't the early onset of the menopause. I didn't think I needed a birth child and I feel happy about that in my skin.

I was very involved in my partner's children's lives and realised I enjoyed being with young people, helping them to sort things out.

Soon after we were approved as foster carers, two boys aged 10 and 15 moved in with us. Their mother had died of alcoholism the day before. The younger boy was like a cork, bobbing up and down in the sea with no safe haven. The older boy had psychotic episodes and terrified my partner. I had to "gatekeep" the older boy for seven days before a place was found for him in a children's home where the supervision ratio is two adults for every young person.

I knew that I wanted to continue to foster but my relationship with my partner broke down. You both have to want to foster.

Since splitting from my partner, I have tailored my life to being a foster carer, choosing my house because of its light, airy rooms and its position opposite a field. I find it easier to manage on my own. I can be completely consistent for the young person without having to manage other relationships.

What happened to the younger boy?
He stayed with me until he was able to live with his father. This was my most rewarding placement, working at his pace, always looking for ways to restore him emotionally. We visited his dad every week for six months until he was ready to move back. The day I took him to settle with his dad was difficult emotionally but it has turned out to be the right thing for him.

I have learned that eventually when human beings feel safe enough, they can feel empathy, love, forgiveness and a sense of self that is solid. We can expect to succeed and believe that we are lovable and precious.

What happens when a young person first comes to live with you?
Whenever a young person is brought to my house by a social worker, I take them off into the field with a couple of cans of Coke to have a chat about how we are going to live together. For example, I listen to what time they

think they should go to bed and if it is reasonable, I agree to it, but if I find they can't get out of bed in the morning, then I've got my evidence to make it earlier.

It's much better if a young person can accept and agree the routines of the household. I try not to impose things and concentrate on making a child feel safe. I do this through empathy, playfulness and "respectful regard", building the young person's self-esteem and reducing their sense of shame. It is about building a reciprocal relationship. When the young person moves in, it is the start of a human dance. My aim is to be in tune with the young person and remain available to them.

Why do you only foster boys?

I believe this reduces the risk of any allegations from young people living with me. I like to be demonstrative and give hugs when appropriate, so I prefer to look after boys to avoid the risk of an allegation. It's a safety issue for me, especially as a single, lesbian carer.

I think social workers should take more responsibility for placements. They were careless about placing the child who had psychotic episodes with us as new carers. They also nearly placed a girl with me who didn't want to be placed with her brother. I feared she would make an allegation just to get moved. I want my world to be safe for me.

However, I am prepared to take risks if I believe it is in the best interests of the young person. When one of the boys I fostered lost his temper, he would fall to the ground as if he'd been shot. I would get a blanket, sit on the floor and put his head on my lap. It probably would have been frowned on by Social Services but it was what he needed. I'm also not afraid to give a child a hug or peck on the cheek, if appropriate. The training about safer caring can frighten potential carers as it puts barriers between you and the children you are trying to look after. It puts a block on spontaneity. I used to feel awkward in the beginning, knowing that everything is potentially risky, but I think when it is long-term, you should be allowed to trust your instincts.

I also believe that safer caring policies can make it very hard for foster carers who have birth children living in the house. It could create a terrible emotional reaction in foster children if they are treated differently from birth children. The important thing is not to harm children and this includes not damaging them emotionally.

What difference, if any, do you think it has made being a lesbian foster carer?

I believe being a lesbian has had a positive impact on my relationships with the boys I look after – it makes them curious and it's a way in to talk about relationships. I also find it easier as a single carer as I can choose when to tell them about my sexuality.

Birth mothers are less threatened by me and therefore more accepting of my role. I'm a foster carer, not a mum or a dad. I'm not trying to usurp their roles.

I find the young people feel quite safe with me. I'm obviously not trying to be their mum or dad. It takes them out of their box a bit and creates conversations about homophobic jokes and what they think of them. This generation is different. Being gay isn't such a big deal.

I have never experienced any homophobia in my work as a foster carer. I can honestly say that being gay has not been a hindrance.

What advice would you give to people thinking about becoming foster carers?

Anyone considering becoming a foster carer should think about their parenting style and how they would want to raise a child. The time to think about this is not in your living room when a child has moved in already. You also need to think about the impact of fostering on your relationship and family and friends.

If you decide to foster through an agency rather than a local authority, you will usually look after children whom the local authority has not been able to place with its own carers, often as a result of a placement breakdown, so you need to be resilient enough to cope with this.

I think placements often break down because foster carers try to create a "pseudo" family. You have to understand they are other people's children. Kids are hyper-vigilant and pick up on stuff. If you are trying to create a pseudo family, they will feel that. For me, being a foster carer is a job and a way of life.

Can you describe some of the challenging behaviour you have encountered and how you have managed it?

The young people I foster have often displayed extremely challenging behaviour before being placed with me. None of them look good on paper. Examples include cutting themselves and using a tourniquet to increase the blood flow, walking the wrong way down a motorway in dark clothes, or sitting on ledges over a precipice deciding whether to jump.

I believe offering children a sense of emotional permanence is important. They need to know you will be there for them for the long-term. I see myself very much as a therapeutic carer, not replacing a child's family but working alongside them and adding value.

One boy who was placed with me hadn't been to school regularly for two years. I monitored his behaviour closely, logging it daily, and worked out what triggered his challenging behaviour. By identifying this, I have managed to keep him in school for the last six months. I like working therapeutically. What the young people are presenting is representative of how they have been treated; once you understand them you can predict what they are going to do in certain circumstances.

I believe it's important not to be punitive. If I feel like grounding a young person for six months, I know I need some time out!

One morning I had waved one of my boys, Kevin, off to school while still in my dressing gown. Within minutes he had called me from the bus stop saying he needed his passport. Still in my dressing gown, I whizzed round in the car to see the bus he was supposed to be catching with its hazard lights on and him shouting and swearing at the driver. He wanted his passport to prove he was 15 to get the reduced fare. However, the situation had escalated and the driver had called the police, and then had to ask the passengers to get off the bus and catch another one. We had 33 passengers scowling at us but I just touched Kevin lightly on the shoulder and we crossed the road to wait for the police. Kevin had a fear of people not believing him, stemming back to childhood. His mother had learning difficulties and often used to ask strangers for help, and they often didn't believe her.

After I had sorted things out with the police, I took Kevin home and we role-played the situation again with him acting as the bus driver. Kevin realised then that he needed help with his anger. I knew this but I needed evidence.

What other advice would you give to people looking after children?
I find it helpful to repeat stories of shared experiences with looked after children. Having been in care myself, I realise how important this is to children. When I looked after my partner's birth children, I noticed how they loved hearing stories about their past.

I also find using someone else's story a way to bring up tough subjects, for example, describing when someone else was bullied and how they reacted. This enables the young person to join in without feeling threatened.

My advice is to remain available but respect young people if they want time alone. I have noticed that a lot of young people feel unjustly treated, so you are continually trying to restore the injustice they feel. However, I would advocate offering empathy, not sympathy.

Have you had good support from social workers?
Your supervising social worker is pivotal to you being a good carer. I believe foster carers can be shoved to the bottom of the priority pile when other professionals are talking about a young person. Just because you haven't got a degree in social work, your views can be sidelined. But you are the one caring for them every day, so you need good communication between you, your supervisor and the rest of the team.

It can be lonely being a single foster carer. I sometimes don't get enough time to process what has gone on in the day and I can find it a bit isolating. It would be useful for agencies to identify two or three carers who live in the same area and to form small support networks. It would be nice to just pop round for a cup of tea.

And from friends and family?

My family has been very supportive and treated my foster children as members of the family. Most of my friends are social workers so they understand if I have to cancel an arrangement at the last minute.

Have class differences had any impact on your relationship with young people in your care?

I work with the young people's parents to try to improve family relationships. I start with the premise that we have something in common, their son. The last two placements have been from middle- to upper-class families. I found them more judgmental. For example, one of them baulked at me wanting another placement. I haven't taken another placement for eight months in order to bond with their son but I can't sustain our standard of living from my own savings and need another placement.

The bonding has worked well. Their son used to run away and be missing for two to three weeks. He ran away in the first week but has stayed with me ever since. I look for the uniqueness in every child. I see myself as a buffer between the system and the young person.

I've learned a lot about the fragility of the human being and the vulnerability of children. I have had children who are carrying a huge amount of shame about their situation and you have to be very careful because you don't know what you might be triggering for them.

How do you prepare young people for leaving home?

I continue to support young people after they have left my care. Adrian, who had Asperger's, lived with me for about 14 months and left in June 2010. We still see each other every three weeks. We tend to light a fire and sit and chat in the garden. My role with Adrian is still very therapeutic and will remain so for some time. He is a very vulnerable young man. I also meet him for dinner once every six weeks and we go to his grandparents. I've stayed in contact with his advocate.

Simon, who is 16 and living with me now, wants to go to university. I will have to fight to get him adequate funding. When young people become 18, they are no longer considered to be "in care". If they continue in education or training, they can receive financial support through a supported lodging arrangement and a small contribution towards university living expenses. However, as a foster carer, who depends on my income, I can't afford to keep a room available for him during university vacations. I think it is a false economy not to look after young people until they leave education. They will cost the system more if you don't support them at this young age. One day they will probably become mums and dads as well.

I see the ongoing relationship with young people as very important. I think the acceptance that I provide, without judgement or labelling, is the best part of my work. It's a fluid thing, constantly learning about the uniqueness of each young person. All of it has value and eventually is rewarding. I am a part of their journey, providing opportunities for them to have a coherent sense of self and to realise their potential.

Graham and Charlie

Graham, 33, is a lecturer and Charlie, 35, works
night shifts in a factory. They have adopted two
boys, Jamie in 2008 and Liam in 2011. The boys
were both two-and-a-half when they came to live
with Graham and Charlie. They are now six and four.
They have no blood connection. They are all white
British and live in the West Midlands.

Graham tells their story with some additional
contributions from Charlie.

Why did you decide to adopt?

One of the hardest things for me about realising I was gay was thinking that
I wouldn't have kids. I'm the eldest of a big family. Charlie knew he was gay
from an early age and had assumed he wouldn't have children.

Some years ago, a lesbian couple we know asked us if we would have a baby
with them. That sparked off a conversation about having children. By this
stage, we had been together for eight years. We both immediately said that

if we were going to have a child that there's enough children in the world without going out of our way to create one, so we thought adoption was the best route for us.

We gave ourselves a year to think about what it would be like to adopt as a gay couple. We spoke to other parents as well as people who had been adopted and another friend whose mother is a lesbian. Having done our thinking and research, we called Social Services.

How did Social Services respond?

We asked the first social worker who came round for the initial interview how long the whole adoption process would take. She told us that normally it takes between one and two years but because we were an "abnormal family", it would take an abnormally long period of time. That was a bit of a wake-up call.

Despite this we went ahead with the assessment process. The social worker who was appointed to work with us was upfront and said he had never worked with a gay couple before and to tell him if he made any incorrect assumptions. The biggest problem he had was who would take the role of mum or dad, so we asked what do you class as the mother or father role in today's world? We pointed out that straight couples don't necessarily have traditional gender-specific roles with the man going out to work and the mother staying at home. We said we would share roles in the same way as any couple who share the jobs that have to be done.

The other issue was the sex of the child we were going to adopt. When we were filling in the form, which asks you to specify the age and sex of the child you would like to adopt, as well as if you are prepared to adopt children with a whole range of special needs, we couldn't make up our minds about whether we wanted to opt for a girl or a boy. However, our social worker said: 'You couldn't possibly have a girl, how would you buy her clothes?' I'm not being funny but I'm gay, of course I can shop! Dads buy clothes for their daughters and I buy clothes for some of my nieces.

The social worker then asked: 'What happens when she becomes a teenager, how would you be able to give her make-up advice?' Most teenage girls would get that advice from their friends rather than their mothers but in any case we know a couple of make-up artists we could call on to throw a make-up party for the girls. The social worker also asked how we would explain the menstrual cycle. It so happens that I am a biology lecturer, and part of my job is to teach students about the menstrual cycle and hormonal differences! Being of the same sex doesn't automatically mean you are the best person to explain things.

How did you decide on your preferences?
We decided we wanted to adopt a child under the age of five because we thought it would be harder for older children to attach to us. We were also prepared to adopt a child with learning difficulties or who was HIV positive. It was really difficult filling in the form because if you are having a birth child, you accept whatever you have, but you wouldn't choose a disability or a certain health status. When adopting the second time around we were less inclined to tick all the boxes because of the impact on Jamie of having a severely disabled sibling. We didn't want to limit Jamie's life now or leave him with the responsibility of looking after a sibling when we die. It was really hard not ticking some of the boxes but we had to think of Jamie.

What has been your experience of the legal system?
It is so slow! It seems to me that Social Services protect themselves first and put the needs of the children second. For our second adoption, we agreed to foster the child we were hoping to adopt, so we actually went through the foster carer preparation programme. The adoption panel agreed the plan but the fostering panel refused to even see us – even though we had been given an appointment – as the panel had no experience of concurrent fostering and adoption and wasn't willing to review our case, so it fell through. It was very annoying in terms of time wasted but also that they weren't willing to talk to us or consider concurrency, which would be much better for children with a good chance of being adopted.

What was it like when you first met the children?

Jamie was the youngest of six and was placed in foster care at nine months old. He lived there for two-and-a-half years and then moved in with us. The reports said that he was a "damaged" child and would never be able to read, had all sorts of learning difficulties and problems with communication. In fact, three years on, he hasn't got any of those. He is top of the class in reading and has performed in a play in our biggest local theatre!

Jamie had formed a strong attachment to his foster family and was able to transfer that attachment to us quite easily. The very first second he saw us he claimed us as his parents. We had sent videos of ourselves before we met Jamie. When we went to meet him he immediately recognised us and said 'Hi Daddy Graham and Daddy Charlie'. We got on like a house on fire. On the third day of introductions, we were due at the foster home at seven in the morning and when we arrived, Jamie and his foster dad were out on the street because Jamie couldn't wait to see us.

Our second adopted child, Liam, was with his birth mother for the first two years but was removed into emergency care, which was meant to be short-term. It turned out to be a more permanent plan, so he moved from respite foster care, to short-term, then to long-term, living with three foster families during a six-month period before he moved in with us.

He hadn't formed an attachment with his mother and did not form an attachment with us very easily. He would play with us but we had to work on trust issues. We had to go right back to letting him be a baby. We instigated an afternoon nap for him, where we would take our shirts off and let him have skin to skin contact and a nap. It did feel silly, we thought what are people going to think? But it worked. After a couple of weeks, he would say, 'I'm tired now, shirt off Daddy'. After about a month, he grew out of it but the relationship changed from that point onwards. Regressing with children and letting them do things that they never had a chance to do before really helps. We also do a lot of role-play, saying things like, 'If you lived here as a baby, then this is what we would do for you'. This works really well and is something we still do with both boys from time to time.

Drinking was also an issue for Liam. His mother tried to stop giving him bottles from the age of about two months and just gave him solid foods. We were told by his last foster carers that if you give him a drink, he would drink the whole thing in one, so they limited his drinks. To me, this exacerbated the problem. They were concerned about him wetting himself but I was less bothered about that and more concerned about him realising that drink was freely available. So we let him have a drink whenever he wanted one and then encouraged him to take a breath and put the drink down for a second. He has now broken that habit as he knows he can get a drink whenever he likes.

I think his foster carers just tried to deal with him on a day-to-day basis, whereas he needed someone to look at his past, understand where the behaviour was coming from, and then plan for his future.

Were there any disappointments?

I think the adoption approval process is good because it makes you question what you are doing and why, but I think it's unnecessarily long. We started the process with eight couples and we were the first to be approved and matched, but even then it took about 12 months. And most of that 12 months was about waiting. You have a meeting every six weeks but nothing seems to happen in between. It is just frustrating. Some of the conversations we had were also pointless.

The second time we went through the adoption approval process, it took even longer, despite the fact that Social Services use us to train prospective adopters, so they must think we are doing a good job. They have also asked us to talk on the radio about our experiences and to speak to potential adopters, so surely the second time around didn't need to take so long?

I was also really disappointed that Social Services seemed to prioritise self-preservation over Liam's needs when a problem occurred. Two days before the matching panel, we were told by the paediatrician that because of his "abnormal" facial features there was an outside chance that Liam had a life-limiting illness so he may end up being severely disabled as a teenager.

The panel wanted to know our reaction to this news. Although we had not wanted a disabled child, we had already made up our minds about Liam so it was too late to turn back, especially as we had already told Jamie about him. That was the point of no return for us. We had already accepted him as part of our family. However, the panel said how would you cope with a 15-year-old who was severely disabled? We said, how do we know? We have never done it before.

So the panel agreed we were still the right match but the panel's boss put a stop on it and said that Liam couldn't move in with us until the test results had come back to verify whether he had the disease.

I was really upset by this. Liam had already been told about us. I couldn't believe they were now delaying it. Even though he was only two, on one day he's told there's a family waiting for him, then he goes for a blood test and then the next day he's told 'Oh no, that family's not ready yet and may or may not have you'. I didn't want him thinking, when he's a teenager, that we put a stop to it, pending the tests.

We were told that the tests would take three weeks but I rang the laboratory directly and the results, which were negative, came back the next day. I don't actually think he has abnormal facial features. I think the paperwork behind these children is disappointing because they are going to see these records one day. Jamie has got blond hair, blue eyes, he's a beautiful boy. The description in his paperwork was that he was short, overweight and had bald patches on his head. It was just awful.

And any surprises?
We were surprised how easy it is to be parents, if you just respond to your child rather than expecting them to respond to you. Loads of our friends had said it is really hard, it will change your life, it will be really difficult. There was quite a lot of negativity. The training course didn't help. It was three days of describing the behaviour you can expect from children who have been physically or sexually abused or neglected and you come away thinking, how are we possibly going to cope with this? In reality, most children don't have all the issues they outlined and even the problems we did face with our

children were fairly easily overcome, and we were often able to come up with fun ways to work them out. Both of our children have had issues to do with their background but they haven't been insurmountable.

Another big surprise was when Jamie first came to the house. Every room was designed for Jamie with toys in each one. Most three-year-olds would have gone ballistic whereas Jamie ignored all the toys and went straight to his pants and socks drawer and said: 'Are these my socks and pants?' When we said yes, he said 'I've never had my own pants before'. At the foster home, because there were so many children coming in and out, they just had communal clothes. So we spent an hour and a half putting all the pants and socks on his head and arms. It was nice in a way but upsetting as well.

It was much harder when Liam moved in. Having two children was a much bigger shock to the system than having one.

What has worked well for you?
Everything, we are very happy with both of our children.

The best thing social workers did was put us in touch with other couples who have adopted. We meet up fairly regularly and we don't talk about adoption all the time but it is nice to talk about some issues with them. It is good for the kids to grow up knowing each other so they aren't the only adopted children in the community. We didn't want them to think they were the only ones. Being gay, we know what that feels like. I remember feeling isolated and desperate, like I couldn't talk to anybody about it when I first came out.

Although it's sometimes easy to find fault with social workers, they are just doing their job and in the end we owe them our family, so they have obviously done a very positive thing for us.

Has it made any difference being gay parents?
I think it's made a huge difference. Having questioned who we are as teenagers, we are more confident now in ourselves which allows us to be the parents the children need. The process of coming out, especially as a

Catholic, meant I had to question every aspect of my life, every aspect of what I thought was true, what I thought about myself. It took about three to four years but at the end of it I was a much stronger person, and I think that has made me a much better parent.

We also know what it's like having disapproving parents and how damaging that can be. We know how important it is to accept your children for who they are. It doesn't matter to us if they have a different take on life as long as they have certain core values, such as being respectful and not hurting anybody.

I also think we can be more creative as dads – we don't have to conform to a stereotypical male role model. All children who have been through the care system need an emotional connection. Being theatrical has helped. Because our children have had so many years of being ignored and not having an emotional connection, it is important to help them recognise and bring out their emotions. By acting and pulling faces we can help them to identify positive and negative feelings.

Another advantage of being a gay couple is that the children's birth parents don't always feel so threatened. We believe that Jamie's mother approved of us as adopters because we were not replacing her. When we met Jamie's mother, we told her he would never have another mother and she was really positive about that. It allows her a place in Jamie's future. Jamie didn't have a father named on his birth certificate. It is easier that we are a brand new relationship. We know Jamie can talk to us about his mum. We don't get funny about it and her letters are really inclusive of us.

As gay parents it is much harder to pretend the children aren't adopted. In any case, I think it's much better to be upfront about it. I know some parents who try to hide the fact their children are adopted. We say yes, we are gay, yes, the children are adopted, and that stops any gossip. In fact, all of our community, school and church see how happy our children are with us and they are all very accepting of our family unit.

In terms of names, at first we tried Daddy Graham and Daddy Charlie but found that didn't work. My dad has always been known by other children in the family as Grandad and Charlie's dad as Grandpop, so one day after about six weeks, we suggested to Jamie that he call us Dad and Pop. Jamie picked up on it straight away but asked what we were going to call him. So we said we'll call you son. He replied: 'If I'm the son, who's the moon?' When Liam moved in, he referred to him as the moon.

About 18 months ago, Jamie got upset, saying he wanted his mum to go into school. Charlie stopped the car immediately to talk to him about it. We honestly don't think it was because he misses his mum because he never really knew her and doesn't get anxious or upset by photos or letters from her. We think it was because other children were saying, where's your mum? So we gave him a photo of his mum to take into school.

Charlie volunteers at the school, which we believe really helps with our integration as a family. If other children like you, it's hard for their parents not to like you or to be worried about you. The whole of Jamie's school calls Charlie, Pop. Quite a few of the kids are jealous that they haven't got a Pop. So, although Jamie hasn't got a mum who he lives with, he has got a Pop, who no one else has, so that helps.

One of the advantages of gay and lesbian adopters is that it is often a first choice as a way of having children, rather than for straight couples, for whom it can be a last resort after trying to get pregnant, possibly through years of IVF.

Have you experienced any homophobia?

We haven't had any negative issues about being gay parents. Jamie goes to a Catholic school and we had a word with the teachers and said we are a gay couple and Jamie is adopted, so on Mother's Day don't be embarrassed. He *has* got a mum, so he can make a Mother's Day card and we can post it off to her. He can talk about being adopted, it's not a secret. Our only issue was the teachers assuming something about Jamie's past and trying to make up for it. I think they had too much sympathy for him and by over-compensating, they singled him out. He was always getting badges every time he did something right and actually we just wanted him to be treated like a normal child.

I have to admit I'm sometimes more conscious of whether our children will turn out gay than I should be because I don't want to fit other people's stereotypes or expectations. For example, I'm more conscious when our sons play typically girlish games than other parents might be. It's silly really.

It's funny, people often think we are good people because we have adopted; actually it was for selfish reasons, because we wanted a family.

What have you learned about yourselves?

I think this is the life I always wanted, whereas Charlie never thought he could have kids and didn't think he'd be a good parent, so I think he's learned that there is much more to him than he used to think.

Charlie jokes: 'I'm less of a human and more of a slave! I can multi-task, I've got more patience, more understanding and am able to put others first. Because they have had such a poor start in life, it's about making sure that you give them time.'

How suportive have friends and family been?

Some of our friends stopped visiting when we had children, probably because they thought we would be too busy or they just didn't know how to deal with kids themselves. However, we have also met a lot of new people through having children. Charlie doesn't speak to any of his family, who kicked him out when he was a teenager, but my parents have been very supportive and were approved by Social Services as babysitters from the start. When Jamie first came to visit our house, my mother was desperate to see him but we said it was too early, so she asked a neighbour if she could look out of their window to catch a glimpse of him in the garden.

It was difficult to leave Jamie with my mum and dad the first time when we went out for an evening. He got upset but it was a good lesson for him that we do come back. The next week he was better. It's about building trust. When we tried a sleepover at my parents, he was excited, packing his bag and special toys, but my mum said he wouldn't go to sleep and at six in the morning he had packed his bag and was waiting by the front door.

We also tried renting a cottage near my sister and letting him have a sleepover there, but again he was awake at six asking for us. With Liam it was easier as he always had Jamie with him.

Our street was hilarious! When Jamie moved in, the neighbours started painting their adjoining fence so they could pop their head over to ask how it was going. The first time we walked down the road with Jamie, both the neighbours opposite came out and started walking to the shop asking how it was going. Once we said it was going well, they turned round again and went back home; they blatantly weren't even going to the shop!

Have you had any external paid help?

I would love to have someone do the ironing. I would strongly recommend one of you gives up work. Charlie changed his full-time day job to working two nights a week to have some adult conversation and get out of the house. This means there is always someone at home for the children.

Charlie says: 'This makes a huge difference. It helps alleviate the stress in the house. I think children in the care system need that stability more than birth children. I also recommend having a babysitter from time-to-time.'

What has been the effect on your finances?

Our expenditure has increased and our income has decreased particularly as Charlie has gone from working full-time to part-time, but actually we now save more because we are more careful. We used to eat out more, have take-aways and just bought stuff without thinking about it. Now we tend to plan our finances, we plan our meals for the week, write a shopping list and stick to it. We still have a takeaway once a month.

What about your work?

As well as Charlie's changes, I used to have two part-time jobs, one at a hospital and one at a university. They both wanted me to go full-time. It was hard to leave the job at the hospital, but the university job was more flexible. I can do more marking at home and I can also work at home during the summer holidays.

What impact has it had on your relationship?

I tend to be more outgoing and Charlie is quieter and less trusting because of his own experiences. When Jamie moved in, I had nine months' leave and Charlie had two weeks and carried on working full-time while I was on adoption leave. Charlie was happy for me to be the main carer in the beginning and we worked well together. The second time was much harder. We had a lot more arguments. I think it was partly because we were both at home full-time as I had three months' adoption leave and by that time Charlie was only working two nights a week. We both work differently around the house. I would get everything done in the morning and spend the afternoon having more fun, while Charlie works at a slower pace.

I guess I wanted to rule the house again and Charlie felt I was pushing him out of place. I hadn't really noticed how long it had taken for Charlie to bond with Jamie but it was much more noticeable with Liam. I bonded instantly but I could see it was hard for Charlie. I would suggest him putting his arm around Liam but Charlie thought I was having a go at him. Time and patience were the biggest healers.

With two children we have far less time to ourselves, so it is harder to sort out issues. The first six weeks were really tough. We didn't let anyone help us even though my parents had been approved by Social Services. After six weeks we let them babysit and went out for a meal. You have to remember to make time for each other. Like all couples we sometimes argue. When we do it in front of the children we tell them afterwards that we still love each other and that neither of us is angry with them. Children can pick up on different moods and things about the house and so we don't want them to get worried or anxious, not knowing what has caused it. Also, showing them that it is OK to have an argument and the different ways people deal with stress in real life are both important lessons.

However, I think it is really important not to disagree about parenting in front of the children. Wait until they have gone to bed to sort out any differences on that front. The children need consistency. They will try to play one off against the other so it is important not to overrule each other or do the "wait until your father comes home" routine. You both need to share responsibility for discipline and rewards. We are constantly discussing our parenting styles with each other.

What part does religion play in your lives?

We take both children to our local Catholic church. We have baptised Jamie, although initially the priest was unsure, not because we are gay, but because we are not married in the eyes of God, even though we are civil partners. The priest ended up having to talk to the archbishop who agreed to the baptism. It was a very special occasion, more of a celebration of Jamie's life than it would have been if he'd been baptised at birth and it was the first time all of his new "forever family" got together to welcome him into our lives; there were probably about 50 of us there.

We find going to church provides us with a good space to have quiet time. It was hard for Jamie to settle down after the first six months of letting him have fun. At church everyone has to be quiet. Jamie sits on our knees and gives us hugs. He also goes to Sunday school and meets other children, which is good for his social skills. I think quite a lot of the teaching is useful for life, for example, about forgiveness and acceptance.

Both our children also light candles once a month at church for their birth families. When asked who they want to light a candle for, they usually say one of their forever cousins or a family pet, but we remind them to say a few words for their mums as well. We think this will help them in the future; they have not forgotten where they came from and are beginning to learn to forgive their birth families already.

Have you had any issues with food?

We used to have a lot of takeaways and not really think about food. Since we've had children, we have had to think more about nutrition, getting a balance of protein and carbohydrates. We always have a big bowl of fruit and salad on the table. They love fruit. We don't force them to eat anything but we like them to at least try new things. It's important to have family meal times.

Liam seems to be hungry all the time and is always asking for more food. Because we know he used to have limited access to food we didn't really want to restrict what he eats because we thought this would exacerbate the problem. So instead we always have a few healthy options available. For example, he can eat grapes and raisins all day long whenever he wants. We also encourage him to get them himself so he knows a shortage of food really isn't a problem here.

How do you feel about not being a birth parent?

We couldn't love our children any more if they were our birth children. I slightly regret not knowing their first words or seeing when they started crawling. However, they already have similar characteristics to us and use our expressions and laughs. I think if anything not being their birth parent allows you to see them for who they are, let them be who they are, and draw out their natural strengths. You're not just trying to raise a "mini-me"!

Have you had to deal with challenging behaviour?

Initially, Jamie was too well behaved. He was too constrained and it took a while to break him out of that. It is easy to overlook someone being too well behaved. People used to say we were lucky, but actually we were really worried; three-year-olds are meant to be naughty sometimes and make a mess, etc. So we both spent a lot of time being naughty ourselves around the house and telling each other off so he could see that it was OK and nothing bad was going to happen. It took about six months, but now he acts like a normal child of his age.

We also had some issues with bath time as Jamie initially had a phobia about water, associated with his past experiences when living with his birth mum. His foster carers used to give him a quick shower and got really anxious themselves when it came to "bath" time, which didn't really help. We tackled it by having bath time at the same time every day so it was never a surprise. We always had the door open, so he didn't feel closed in. Because of his fear of water, we got him a wetsuit, flippers and a snorkel along with loads of toys, which provided a distraction, as well as protection for him. Within a week, he had relaxed enough to have a proper bath and quickly started playing in there for up to 20 minutes at a time.

The first time we went swimming, he clung to me for two hours. He didn't scream but he was scared. This lasted for a couple of weeks but now he swims around happily and is confident in the water.

In terms of speech, we were told that Jamie was severely delayed. However, we think he was talking too quickly so it came out garbled, so we tried slowing him down and his speech has improved hugely. We were also told by the foster carers that we should read with him for 10 minutes a day. This used to be a battle as they forced him to sit down and read at set times. Instead, we just scattered books around the house and picked them up ourselves and started reading them. This made him curious to see what we were reading. He is now one of the top readers in his class.

Jamie also had trust issues. He would make up injuries to see how we would respond. We entered his world and wrapped him head-to-toe in bandages to show we cared. By us over-exaggerating our response in a childish way, he thought it was funny, learned to trust us and eventually stopped faking the injuries.

With Liam, it was hard at first as he showed no emotional connection. He wouldn't look people in the eyes and his facial muscles hadn't developed. We were told this could be an indication of learning difficulties. In fact, we think it was more to do with neglect. Social workers seem to assume the worst and set low goals. We didn't think it was learning difficulties and thought that actually he was quite bright.

We started doing facial massage with him and reminding him to look in our eyes and playing games like "peek-a-boo" with him to encourage eye contact. We also taught him how to express his feelings through role-play. He now has more of a sparkle in his eyes and more facial expressions. In fact, our social worker commented that his entire face had changed just six weeks after he had moved in with us.

Liam also had some attachment disorder, calling lots of people auntie and going up to anybody he met. He needed more physical contact with us and we gave him kisses and hugs as appropriate, while being mindful of his previous experiences. It is upsetting when you are trying to give a child love and you are faced with a brick wall. You have to deal with this and persevere, remembering that he isn't so much rejecting you as he just simply has no idea how to respond or deal with love. Now he is fine with intimacy and extremely well attached to us and shows appropriate responses to strangers.

Liam also had an obsession with guns. His birth family had guns but the foster family thought they were too violent so banned them. We thought this made him want them even more. We didn't go out and buy a load of guns but would play with a kind of mini-hoover that you use to suck up insects and things as if it were a gun. He also had an issue with potty training. The foster family had shouted at him for wetting himself. We put a nappy on him and waited until he wanted to wear pants. If he had an accident we just said, you have to get to the toilet more quickly. When he used the potty we sang a song and danced to make it a fun thing to celebrate.

Have you had to deal with sibling rivalry?
We did have some sibling rivalry when Liam moved in, even though we had prepared Jamie as much as possible. I'd asked Jamie what he was looking forward to and what he was scared about. I'd also said that I was scared I wouldn't spend as much time with Jamie and he would think I didn't love him. Jamie replied: 'Don't be ridiculous, you'll always love me.'

The first thing Jamie said to Liam was: 'Hello, I'm your forever brother'. Liam instantly recognised him from the videos we had given to the foster family.

For Jamie, there wasn't much of a warning period, as you would get with a baby growing up in the family; he just suddenly had a two-year-old brother taking his toys and playing roughly. We agreed to hide some toys and to share some. You need to take an active role in their relationship and tend it like a garden. We let them bathe together but are always in the vicinity to make sure nothing inappropriate happens. We tell them how to be brothers and allay their fears when they don't really understand why one or the other has done something to upset the other. That said, they always got on from the start. And now, if we tell one of them off the other will scold us for shouting at their brother! They are very protective of each other.

How have you managed setting boundaries, rewards and sanctions?

The hardest thing about boundaries is following our own rules, for example, remembering to take your shoes off or holding on to the banister when going downstairs. We don't believe in the naughty corner or step. If children have a negative impression of themselves then that might reinforce it. We have time out and the children have to sit quietly with us for two minutes, usually on our knees. We don't say 'sit there because you have been naughty', but rather 'you need a little time out to calm down a little bit and think about what you are doing'. They are still being punished but we have not called them naughty, left them on their own or separated them from where they were. They normally get upset and we give them a hug afterwards.

We are careful about not taking toys away as a punishment. Liam's toys are sacrosanct. These children have already had so much taken away from them that we want them to begin to trust that this won't start happening again. We have sometimes banned playing on the Wii as a punishment. They usually get three warnings and then it is banned, not just for them, but for us as well. Sometimes, however, I do shout at them.

In terms of rewards, we don't have stickers or anything like that. We usually have hugs or happy dances. Most of Jamie's bad behaviour is to do with losing games. We have role-played losing at a game ourselves and having a strop to show him what it is like. It's funny, then he says to us: 'Calm down Dad, it's OK, I'll let you win next time'.

Another behaviour issue we had with Liam was his independence. He didn't know what a parent should be like so tried to do everything for himself. It's a fine line to tread because you want your children to grow up into independent adults, but you also need to teach them some co-dependency. We would say things like, 'I can help you with that because that's what dads do'.

What has worked well in terms of activities?

We have found dancing and drama have been good, as they give the children a useful way of expressing their emotions and building their confidence.

Jamie had a problem with his handwriting, so we gave him chalk to draw on the paving slabs in the garden. You can also use shaving foam, which helps them to create shapes while holding something. Charlie hooked up a projector to the computer and the stylus pen then projected what he was writing on to the wall. Jamie loved that. We also started a diary, which he likes. You have to use your imagination and try out different things to find out what works for them.

Other activities that have worked well include indoor climbing, games, karaoke, dancing, junior Scrabble, table football and Beavers. When Jamie first moved in we banned computers and DS. We got quite a lot of stick for this from other parents and family members but we feel they just suck children in and require them to spend hours on their own. Once he was six, we gave Jamie a DS. He had wanted one for three years but at least he had learned to play with us. We also bought a Wii as at least we can all play on this together as a family. A lot of children Jamie's age have a TV in their room but we don't want them to spend time by themselves, so again we haven't gone for this.

How have you explained the children's pasts to them?

I think it's easier, being a gay couple, to explain the children's pasts. There is no hiding from the fact that you aren't their natural mum and dad. For straight couples, they can have the best of intentions but sometimes forget to explain the children's pasts, particularly if there is no birth family contact. Time can just race by.

We have photos of the children's birth families and we thought of putting them on the living room wall at first, but then we realised that we would have to explain them to new friends when they came into our home and this would be an invasion of our children's privacy too. So instead we keep these pictures on the computer and the boys can ask to look at them at any time. We also light a candle at church for their birth families and say a prayer for them, hoping they are safe and well. We write letters twice a year and let Jamie and Liam choose the photos they want to send to their birth families. In the garden, we have planted some flowers as a reminder of their birth mothers.

On Mother's Day, they both write cards to their mums and we put them up in our house for about a month to show them that we are all thinking about them before sending them off to their birth families. We have reminded the school about this and asked them to let us know if they mention their birth families. Before Liam moved in, we went into Jamie's school to speak to the teacher. The school decided to hold a special family day where they explained all sorts of different family units, including foster families and forever families. This helped Jamie's classmates understand why his new brother was going to be two years old instead of a baby and showed Jamie that his teachers and friends accepted his family unit.

I think it's important to be honest about the children's pasts. I found out that my dad wasn't my real dad when I was 14. My birth father had abused my mother and been in and out of prison for drug dealing, and my mother had remarried. She led me to believe that my stepfather was my real dad. He left when I was six. When I was 14, my real dad turned up drunk. I felt like the bottom of my world had fallen away, I knew who he must have been because he was my double. I was very scared I'd turn out like him, I could literally feel his blood running through my veins, and my mum was scared I'd want to be in touch with him. I became extremely frightened, angry and confused for several years. Feeling unable to talk about this to anybody in my family only made it worse.

Then one day one of my aunties told me that my mum and dad were in love when they had me. This was a turning point for me. I went to visit my dad in prison. It was touching. He said never to follow his example, he'd made bad choices, it might sound exciting breaking the law but it's not, it's just really lonely. He said he was very proud of me going to college and that I was the only good thing he'd done in his life. For a man who had no idea how to be a father, this was pretty good advice.

My mum had a huge go at me for visiting him. So, I decided to cut off contact although I felt sorry for my birth dad because he really didn't have anybody in his life. That is my only regret. Every year, I perform in a show at our local theatre and one year, in the interval, a woman came up to me and said she recognised me because I look so much like my real dad. She was my dad's sister, and asked me to give my mum her number. I said, she is unlikely to call you, so she said: 'If it helps, your dad died a couple of months ago'.

This experience definitely influences my decision about keeping open lines of communication with the children's birth families. We will support them if they want to see their parents when they are older, as long as they understand that although their birth families love them, they do not know how to live safe lives and so our children can love them back, but should not expect too much from them or trust their way of life. It is important that they know there has always been love in their lives and there are reasons why their birth families grew up into people unable to properly look after their children or to keep them safe.

We will tell them things about their parents as they become old enough to understand. At the moment, we say your mum loves you but couldn't look after you and keep you safe and there were some dangerous people in your life and your mum couldn't protect you from them.

Would you adopt or foster more children?

We would consider adopting more children but would need financial assistance to find a big enough house. I believe we could look after four children, from an emotional point of view. Another option is fostering but we would only foster children younger than our youngest child. If we did have any more children we would opt for girls so the boys would have sisters.

We believe the mortgages and housing schemes available to key workers should be extended to adopters and foster carers. This would help more families provide permanent homes for children in the care system.

What advice would you give to people thinking of adopting?

Seriously question why you want to do it. Are you prepared to take on a child who may not fit your ideal of how a child should be? Once you have got your head around that I would definitely recommend it. It has changed our lives for the better.

What advice would you give to social workers?

Social workers should try to give a balanced view of the children in care, not just the extreme cases. There is often a stigma attached to children in care and most of the prejudice is wrong. Even really damaged children have good days. And let's face it, some birth children display extremely challenging behaviour.

Widen your horizons about the types of families you are looking for, for example, if someone smokes one cigar a month, they should not be prohibited from adopting so long as they don't do this in front of the children, of course.

Loosen the rules so that adopters can get key worker benefits, otherwise it is only middle-class people who can afford to adopt. We were also told that only blood relations could share a room, even though both children had shared rooms in their foster homes and many siblings share rooms.

What are your greatest achievements?

Charlie says: 'We have taken the children out of awful situations and given them the best chance possible.'

I think we are good at seeing the children for who they are without any of the baggage parents sometimes have, wanting them to be like them. We also don't feel any pressure to conform to targets, for example, potty training your child by a certain time.

Charlie adds: 'You have to go at the pace of the children and not force them to do anything, like saying I love you, until they are ready.'

Last year Jamie and I were on the radio talking about adoption for National Adoption Week. Jamie was asked what it was like to be adopted. He said: 'Being adopted means that when I grow up and have kids, my Dad and Pop can look after them.' Although we all go into adoption for selfish reasons – wanting a family of our own – you do quickly realise that it is not just your child whose life you are changing, but also their children's, and their children's children. This is a very humbling feeling and providing these kind of life-changing opportunities is our greatest achievement.

Jamie, aged six

What is the best thing about living here?

The best thing is opening presents. A cheetah and a chipmunk are my
best toys.

(Jamie received the cheetah when he went to court to be adopted and
the chipmunk when Liam was adopted. He has got hundreds of teddies but
cheetah goes everywhere with him.)

How did you feel when Liam moved in?

Sad because he pushes me over.

What was the first thing you said when you met Liam?

You have a big brother now.

What did you do when Liam first came to your school?

I picked him up and took him into Year 2 to show my friends.

Do you like having a Pop and a Dad?

Yes, I love them.

And what will it be like when you are older?

They can come to my house, paint my house and look after my children.

How many children are you going to have?

Five or four.

What are you looking forward to?

Going to the park and playing on the slide.

What else?

Going on the London Eye.

12 Mark and Kieran

Mark, 45, a support worker for adults, and his partner, Kieran, 42, a hairdresser, have been together for eight years. They fostered Will three years ago, when he was 14. They live together in London. They are all white British.

Mark tells their story.

Why did you decide to foster?

I saw an advertisement in our local newspaper and chatted the idea over with Kieran. We decided to give each other space to think about it. The initial reason was to give a young person a better start in life. We went to an open evening and found out more about it but until you actually foster, you don't realise the amount of time it takes and the impact it has on your life.

We thought long-term fostering would offer a young person stability. We wanted them to live with us on a permanent basis and to fit into our family unit. We thought we could offer consistency and build up a relationship with a young person. We didn't want to foster short-term and, having built up a rapport, see the person leave.

How did you find the approval process?

The assessment took almost a year and then we decided to have a cooling-off period to give us a chance to step back and think about it. Our link worker was great about this. Anyway, after a while we decided to go ahead with it. Our social worker then said she had someone in mind, so the next step involved meeting Will's social worker and then we moved towards introductions.

What was it like when Will moved in?

We had a honeymoon period. His last placement was in the countryside, so it was a contrast to live in a city. Previously, he travelled by taxi to his old school but he didn't like having to get up so early. Two years ago, we moved him into a local school, which is much better. The school was very up-to-date and had a specialist in looked after children. We have helped Will make new friends. It was a really big transition for him but we were all keen for it to happen. For any young person in care, change presents difficulties but he coped really well.

After the honeymoon period, which lasted about four weeks, Will had a few problems with anger management, so we had to deal with this. We spoke to him and dealt with the problems head-on. We told him that it was fine to express his anger but that it was inappropriate to damage himself, other people or property.

We find humour defuses a lot of situations. You also have to have empathy and be willing to listen. I have worked in a children's home, with homeless people and adults with learning difficulties, so I find this experience helps.

You have to try to put yourself in their shoes. They have been moved around and don't feel settled. They won't have respect for a home until they feel settled, so you need to offer stability, security and consistency.

Have you experienced any homophobia or negativity?

Kieran and I kiss each other goodbye and Will doesn't bat an eyelid. His social worker asked him how he felt about living with a gay couple and he said he didn't know any gay people but he seems chilled out about it.

Some of my gay friends asked why we wanted to do it, and some admitted they couldn't do it, but not everyone wants a family. Most of our friends accept what we have done.

What have you learned about yourself?

I have more patience than I thought. I enjoy being with young people and have come to accept that they have different attitudes and likes and dislikes.

Does Will have contact with his birth family?

He has contact with his father and brothers. In the beginning, I felt a bit awkward speaking to his dad on the phone. I've never actually met him but when Will broke his collarbone I had to call him and he appreciated me contacting him. We are a big part of Will's life and so is his dad.

What has been your experience of social workers?

We felt supported at the beginning of the placement. As Will isn't presenting any problems, his social worker has left us to it. She visits periodically, perhaps every three months. Our supervising social worker also visits every three months.

What impact has fostering had on your lives?

It has had a big impact. Until we started fostering, we didn't realise what a difference it would make. Before a child or young person is in your life, you only have to think about you and your partner. Now we have to plan things much more, always make sure someone is at home at tea time, there is food in the house, and so on. We have had to be methodical but once you get into it things become more normal.

However, now that Will is a bit older, we are encouraging him to learn some life skills and do some cooking for himself.

There are a lot of meetings to organise, Personal Educational Plans (PEPs), Looked After Children (LAC) reviews, etc. This used to be a pain but now we are used to it.

What advice would you give regarding managing boundaries, rewards, sanctions, etc?
We are not strict parents. We have set some boundaries, saying this is what we want or expect you to do. We are flexible – as long as he lets us know where he is and why. He will be finishing school soon, so we need to allow him some freedom.

What has been your experience of holidays?
We went to Turkey, which was the first time Will had been abroad. We also went to a festival with him. It is great to get away.

Have you had any respite care?
We had about four days' respite when we went to Wales for a few days. Will went to another foster carer but was glad when we got home.

What has been your experience of activities?
We go to the cinema quite a lot, as well as bowling and go-karting, and he plays on his PlayStation 3. Will is quite active and enjoys cycling.

How are you preparing Will for leaving home?
As he is 17, in theory, he could leave now if he wanted to. The foster placement officially comes to an end when he is 18 but we have said he doesn't have to leave. We are encouraging him to be independent in terms of doing his own washing, trying to encourage him to cook and learn some budgeting skills. He has saved his pocket money and contributed towards the music festival.

He has opened his own bank account and we have shown him household bills and the mortgage, so he is more familiar with these things when and if he has his own home, but we are not rushing him out the door.

What advice would you give to people thinking about fostering?

Think long and hard before committing yourself and be realistic and serious about it. It is well worth doing and there is so much need in society as there are so many kids in care. If you put a lot in, you get a lot out.

Will, aged 17

What is it like living with Mark and Kieran?

I was living with a straight, married foster couple before. They were quite old and they blamed me for their stuff. I was also in the countryside, so I couldn't go out with friends so easily. It is a lot better here.

I went to Turkey with Kieran and Mark, which was the first time I'd ever been abroad. I've also been go-karting and to the cinema. They treat me like their son, it's like a family.

I can talk to them about girls and male things. We have a laugh. They are good at listening and give me space when I need it.

How did you react when social workers asked if you wanted to live with them?

When I first heard I was moving in with a gay couple I was a bit uncertain, so I spoke to my dad. He told me to see if they were nice people and find out if I liked them.

Have you experienced any homophobia?

When I started at school, it was all OK, but after three or four months they found out that I was living with gay foster carers. They took the piss out of me and it spread around the school. Mark and Kieran told the school and they got onto the case. It was sorted out after that. The person who started it got detention.

What do you want to do in the future?

I want to go to college and try to get a job. I want to do art and design and become a graphic designer, probably of billboards. The college is down the road. I'm happy to stay here until they say "get out"!

13   Kate and Sophie

Kate, 38, and Sophie, 40, adopted two siblings,
Carly, aged four, and Ryan, aged five. They are now
eight and nine. Kate used to be a copywriter but is
now a full-time mother and Sophie is a lawyer. They
are all white British and live in the North West of
England.

Kate tells their story.

Why did you decide to adopt?

We wanted a family. We tried sperm donation from a friend, which didn't
work. To be honest, we were a bit uncertain about what it would be like with
four parents being involved. We also tried IVF. Now we are glad it didn't work
out. Sophie wanted to carry a baby but I never wanted to.

I'd always fancied adoption but friends tried to discourage us and initially
the application forms put us off. We also went to an open evening run by a

foundation where one of the women said her favourite part was going into people's houses and being nosey!

Later on, we received something from the council by chance, that had a postage advert on it saying, 'Could you adopt?' Around that time, I also saw an advertisement on the back of a bus and read an article in *The Guardian* newspaper. This all prompted us to go to another open evening. Thirteen months later our children moved in.

How did you find the application and assessment process?
The process was quite easy. I think if you go into it with a positive attitude, it helps. We were open and enjoyed the training courses. We made some good friends. There were two gay men on the course but they didn't make it past the training.

Generally, we sailed through it and were allocated a lovely social worker. There were one or two moments when I felt like a jellyfish, answering questions that made me feel awkward. You have to accept that social workers are doing their job and have to get it right. To speed things up, I think there should be more social workers and faster court proceedings.

During our application process, we were under the impression that there were very few babies but I have been on the local adoption panel for two years and there are lots of babies. Luckily, neither of us craved the baby experience.

Going to panel was very stressful – it was like being in a pressure cooker.

How did you decide on the age range?
Initially, we wanted two children aged three to six but we met a girl who had been adopted at eight and she persuaded us to extend the age range to eight. In fact the children were five and four when we adopted them.

What was it like when they moved in?
We were told that Ryan had already been in therapy for years and that nobody could understand what had gone on in his life. We were also told

that he would have lengthy screaming episodes. When he walked through our door, his shoulders literally dropped an inch. He still plays up but he is nowhere near as problematic. We had more difficulty with Carly. It took nine months before she could trust us.

We had to keep reassuring them that this was their house and that stuff in the drawers belonged to them.

They both loved being able to choose how their bedrooms were decorated and liked being the only children in the family. Previously, they were in a foster family for three years with two other foster children and a birth child. They knew they weren't treated the same as the birth child.

Can you describe some of the challenges you have had to face?
All families have to deal with challenging behaviour. It is difficult to know if it is because of the children's past or if it is just natural for their age. For example, Ryan can be mean to Carly – now is this sibling rivalry, to do with their history, or something else happening at school? Historically, Ryan was favoured and Carly almost starved to death, so obviously, that could be the explanation.

I had to restrain Ryan once because he was kicking and screaming. He gets a look in his eye and just stares at you. It seems to happen every three months. It may be linked to stuff going on at school. Ryan is not very academic because he missed out on school before he moved in with us.

Ryan has loads of energy so you have to find ways of getting rid of that. It is harder when it rains. For example, one day in half-term, we had done loads of stuff but by eight in the evening, we all needed time out away from each other. Sometimes, they can drive me mental. Other times they can be very loving and adorable. Ryan writes little notes saying, 'I love my mums'.

For the first nine months, Carly loved Sophie when she came home from work but hated me, who was the one looking after her at home and, of course, having to tell her off sometimes.

One day, I trapped her finger in the front door, by mistake. We were in a rush to a Hallowe'en party, so she was in fancy dress. We rushed to an NHS walk-in centre but luckily, nothing was broken. When we came home, she sat on my knee and cried and I rocked her. I felt terrible but actually that episode changed things. She realised that I was there for her and was going to look after her. I put on a film and soothed her and we sat there for a couple of hours – just the two of us. There was a look in her eye that day and I knew something had clicked.

They both love living here now. I was brought up in quite impoverished circumstances and I look at them and think they are a lot better off.

We are constantly reassuring them that this is their family. Our password is 'I love you'. We've forgotten almost that they are adopted.

What impact has adoption had on your life?

Life was fantastic before, we both had well-paid jobs, we would go to Florence for a weekend, etc, but it always felt as if something was missing. I remember during the two weeks of introductions, sitting in a family restaurant that we would never have gone to before. I looked over at a young couple without children and thought – you are free. I did have a yearning for our old life then.

In the first few months we used to argue over who would pop out to get milk just to get some time on our own and feel free to stare into space.

Luckily, Sophie and I have a lovely relationship and we support each other. However, we have had to make sacrifices and are nowhere near as frisky as we used to be. We can't just do as we please any more.

Our house used to be like a pristine show home but now we have fingerprints on our Farrow and Ball walls and book bags, tennis rackets and stickers everywhere. The garden is ruined from Ryan playing football.

Holidays now cost a fortune. We went on a five-star holiday to India before the children, while last year we spent the same money on a two-week caravan holiday in the UK.

I used to run a nightclub and have spiky hair and now I'm organising parent/

teacher events and seem very respectable – I can see the funny side of it!

What have you learned about yourself?

I have learned a lot about being a mum. It has opened my eyes to many things and introduced me to a new way of looking at things happening in society, for example, anti-social behaviour – now I might try to understand why it is happening. I realise now how important it is to feel secure. If children's needs are not met, they are going to feel angry.

How do you feel about not being a birth mother?

It doesn't bother me. I never felt the need to give birth. Actually, I feel very proud of the fact that we have adopted, especially as a same-sex couple. I think it is actually easier, as a same-sex couple, to say that you have adopted children rather than giving birth to them, but I hope, in time, that attitudes will change.

In terms of my love for the children, I feel I could stop a train coming towards them with my own body. I don't think I could love a birth child any more than I love them.

What level of contact do you have with their birth family?

We have annual letterbox contact where we exchange a letter and photos. I do find contact tricky. Once you have become attached, every so often you remember that a part of them is linked to other people. Every year around letterbox contact time, we are all sent into a bit of a spin. Their birth mother is quite difficult, writing about the wonderful times they used to have or that we are just looking after them until she is better. We deal with it by being open and honest.

Have you experienced any homophobia?

No. Perhaps because we live in a middle-class area, people are too polite to say, but also we are one of the most conventional, unconventional families you'll ever find. I'm on the Parent/Teacher Association, we have Sunday lunches and I've helped organise a festival parade.

Once I lost my temper on the street – people can criticise me for that but not for the fact that we are two mums bringing up children.

What advice would you give to social workers?

They should view same-sex couples in the same way as straight couples. They should see everyone as individuals and assess them on merit.

What do you think about the media portrayal of same-sex parents?

Why aren't there more positive stories about what is going on in the UK? I read an article in *The Guardian* about same-sex parents and they were nearly all from the US, yet I could name 10 couples within a five-mile radius of me.

I write a blog in which I try to normalise things. You wouldn't necessarily know we are a same-sex couple, although sometimes I mention my co-mummy. I've also written features about our experience.

What would you say to someone thinking of adopting?

It is the best thing I have ever done and gives me a lot of pleasure. However, you really need to think about it, ask yourself about your motivation and your approach to bringing up children. Don't be defensive with social workers and remain open-minded. I think your approach determines how people react to you. Be patient with social workers, sometimes they have to get four or five colleagues around a table to make a decision.

Be excited about what you are doing and keep an eye on the prize; for us it was not only doing a good deed but building a family.

14 James

James, 29, a single, white British care worker, adopted Darren, aged five, a boy with multiple disabilities, three years ago. James' mother also lives with him in a small village in Yorkshire. He has been approved to adopt a second child and is looking for a suitable match.

Why did you decide to adopt?

I worked in a care home when I was about 17 and was told off for interacting with the residents when I should have been cleaning. When I went to work at a residential care home for children and adults with severe learning difficulties, the feeling that something was missing in life disappeared. I started as a care worker and became a senior project worker. The project involved helping the children and adults get out into the community, creating and selling their artwork.

I had a huge desire to become a father and adoption seemed to be the best option. However, I was 25 at the time and I thought, 'They are not going to want me – I'm too young and not rich enough'.

I specifically wanted to adopt a disabled child because of working in the disability field for a long time.

How did the application process go?

I made an initial enquiry and that was very positive, but the whole process took two-and-a-half years. I was deferred at the panel because they said I lacked life experience. However, the independent decision-maker over-ruled the panel. The matching panel also deferred, saying Darren would be better off in a foster home because of his special needs and that I wasn't experienced enough. That was very disheartening because I think I am mature for my age. My father was a vicar, so we were exposed to a lot of different people and their problems while we were growing up. I think because I was the first single, gay man to apply, they were nervous about approving me and although I had worked with children with disabilities, I had never brought up any children.

The second approval has only taken eight months. I'm now well known to Social Services but I also think I am more mature now and think like a father.

And the introductions?

They went on for a month because of Darren's needs. It was incredibly tiring. I used to come home emotionally drained. However, I formed a very close relationship with his foster mother over that time. Her husband died during the introductions and I don't know how she kept going, she was amazing. She has subsequently become Darren's godmother.

How about your support network?

My mother is a great support. She has a separate part of the house and I don't take advantage of her to babysit. If she wants to have her own space she takes herself off. We have also agreed that if it gets too much for her she can move to a warden-controlled flat nearby.

She loves having a grandson and Darren is very aware that she is my mother and not a surrogate mother to him. Social Services were a bit worried about the arrangement, thinking that Darren might think of her as his mother but he knows she is his grandmother.

In terms of other support, I have friends who have been great, all with different qualities. However, you find out who your true friends are when you adopt. I tend to go out with friends who have children. I live in a cul-de-sac and all the neighbours have accepted Darren.

Can you describe him?

Darren has autism and foetal alcohol and Foetal Valproate Syndrome. Foetal Valproate Syndrome is a rare congenital disorder caused by exposure of the foetus to valproic acid, a drug used to control epilepsy, during the first three months of pregnancy. Symptoms may include spina bifida, distinctive facial features, and other musculoskeletal abnormalities. Darren also has a very low immune system, so has had chickenpox three times and septicaemia. However, nothing phases me. He is a child who needs a loving home.

When Darren moved in, he would sit in a corner and wouldn't come near me. Now he is a very sociable child and has come on in leaps and bounds. He has been in a special needs school but is going to a mainstream school in the new academic year. He is such a rewarding child.

How has adoption affected your work?

I used to work full-time at a residential school for children with complex disabilities. Now I work 15 hours a week for a boy in the village who has cerebral palsy. Darren can come with me if he is at home.

I get an adoption allowance for Darren because of his special needs and this may be possible with the second child – that would be a bonus. Luckily, I have savings and I would recommend people save some money before adopting – kids cost a fortune!

What have you learned about yourself?

Adoption has made me a bigger and stronger person. I look at life differently and don't take things so seriously. If my child achieves something it feels 10 times better than if a child without disabilities achieved something.

I love my life now. I know it would be empty without children.

Have you had a relationship since you adopted?
No, I can't really envisage having a relationship. I'm quite content with my life but if someone came along, it would have to be a very slow and steady introduction to our lives.

What will happen when the children are older?
I hope they will move towards having semi-independent lives. In case anything happens to me, I have chosen good godparents – their foster mother and my brother, who is also gay.

What part does religion play in your lives?
I was brought up in a strict religious family, with my father being a vicar. I think religion gives you a set of standards to live by but I don't think you need to have that to be a good adoptive parent. I had Darren christened, which felt like a welcome into our family. It was more of a day of celebration than the day when he was adopted as the adoption ceremony only lasts a couple of minutes.

Do you have any contact with the birth family?
We have letterbox contact with Darren's mother, father and aunt. We get lovely letters from his aunt and exchange photos. His mother is lovely but both parents have paranoid schizophrenia. I met his mother by chance one day, and I gave her a hug and asked if she wanted to hug Darren but she didn't know what to do. I knew then that it was so right for him to be with me.

My mother and father fostered three children whose mother had schizophrenia. I was worried about ticking the box saying I would consider a child with schizophrenia but I don't think you should rule out any disabilities. There are children with a squint who are being ruled out by potential adopters who say no to any disabilities. It is wise to tick the "willing to discuss" box as panels don't take lightly to you saying no to a disability and then saying yes if you are matched because they think you are being pressurised.

When I found out about Darren's parents' history I did some research and found that if it is genetic – there is a 50 per cent chance of his inheriting schizophrenia, but this is reduced to 25 per cent as his father's was brought on by drug addiction. If a child is adopted into a healthy environment then the chances are lessened to 19 per cent. In the end, I decided that if Darren does become schizophrenic then I just need to deal with it. You always have to expect the unexpected and be prepared for uncertainties. You are not going to get a perfect child but you could have a biological child who becomes schizophrenic.

When he is older, he might want to meet his birth parents. I'm totally cool with this. We should be proud that he has birth parents and not shun the fact. However, I'll always know that I'm the parent who has brought him up.

How do you feel about not being a birth parent?

I don't feel any differently, I'm a parent in every way. My son calls me Daddy and he means it from the heart and I call him son and mean that from the heart. Adoption is what you want to make of it. I never say this is my adopted son, I always say, this is my son.

It's bizarre, Darren actually looks like me and is picking up my mannerisms.

What advice would you give about preparing for a child to move in?

Listen to the foster carers. You might not want to follow what they are doing but do it in the beginning, as it is what the child is used to. Try to keep some of the familiar smells in the initial stages. For example, I didn't wash Darren's pyjamas and bed sheets for a week, so he could still have the smell of the foster carers around him – obviously, I would have cleaned them if he'd had an accident. I wouldn't have chosen the clothes he came with but it was important for him to retain some familiarity. You can gradually introduce your own routines and ways of being. We still visit his foster home and he is happy to sit where he used to sit but then when it is time to leave, he knows he's coming home.

Use your introductions wisely but be prepared; it was the most tiring and physically draining time of my life. At the same time, it was very exciting because I was going to visit my son. Usually, I would be at the foster home from 6.30am to be there when Darren woke up through to 9pm. I remember one time coming home and falling asleep on the sofa, still in my clothes.

Don't be afraid to ask the foster carers questions and take a note pad – you can't remember everything. Phone them every night and speak to the child, so they get used to your voice. Give the child a teddy or soft toy, sprayed with your aftershave or perfume, so they get used to your smells. It was strange getting used to being called Daddy and saying my son, it sounded so weird at first.

If you need an extra couple of days before the child moves in, ask for it – Social Services should respect your decision.

What was it like when Darren moved in?
I couldn't say I had undying love for Darren at the beginning. I cared for him but it was hard. He would run away if I sat next to him and I didn't really know how to love him. It is not like you have nine months to bond during a pregnancy.

However, one day, Darren fell over and bumped his head and I rushed over, picked him up and cuddled him and felt an instant love. I thought, 'Oh my God, I love you.' Something had clicked.

What advice would you give about managing challenging behaviour?
If a child is misbehaving, they are just being a child. It is not necessarily because they are adopted. Don't blame their behaviour on "being in care". Obviously, there may be issues related to their past but generally, if a child is writing on a wall, for example, it is because that is what children do.

I don't believe in smacking, I think you can reason or find another way – I have a look now and Darren knows he has done something wrong.

Can you describe some of your activities together?

Darren loves to come out into the garden with me. We go swimming every day in a hydrotherapy pool. Sometimes, we go on a tractor run at a local farm or trampolining, which is good fun. We have a great village community – we often go for a run, go shopping, bump into people we know and generally have a normal family life. We are going to Florida for a holiday and have been to Ibiza recently.

What advice would you give to social workers?

Gay men and lesbians who want to be parents are more likely to accept uncertainty and deal with negativity as they have already experienced this by coming out or facing discrimination. My father wasn't very accepting when I came out at the age of 17 but I had to deal with that.

I think the safer caring policies are a load of rubbish. Of course, you should be able to kiss or cuddle a child. It's about where you draw the line. I'm a parent. I do what a child needs.

What advice would you give to potential adopters?

It is a fantastic thing to do. It is very challenging and like being on a roller coaster but it is very rewarding. Don't ever think Social Services won't want you because you are lesbian or gay. Try to talk to people who have adopted. Call the local authority and ask them to put you in touch with someone in your area. This way the panel will see that you have taken some of the right steps to prepare yourself. Be prepared for a long wait, adoption won't happen overnight. Read plenty of books. Keep in contact with the people on your preparation course.

Overall, it is a fantastic opportunity and process – the whole thing is amazing.

Tina and Claire

Tina, 43, a white Irish civil servant and Claire, 41, a white Irish teacher, live in Northern Ireland. They have been together for twenty years and wanted to adopt a young child; however, lesbians and gay men in Northern Ireland cannot adopt as a couple. Claire applied to adopt as she has better adoption leave entitlement from her work. She was approved but waited over three years for a match before changing tack.

Claire and Tina were told their chances would increase if they tried long-term fostering with a view to one of them adopting. Lesbians and gay couples are allowed to foster jointly in Northern Ireland. They were approved as foster carers and Laila, a white Irish girl, was placed with them, aged two-and-a-half. She has lived with them for three years and now Claire is hoping to adopt her.

The Human Rights Commission in Northern Ireland recently won a judicial review challenging the ban on unmarried couples adopting. It is not yet clear whether there will be an appeal.

Tina tells their story with some extra comments from Claire.

Why did you want to adopt?

We always wanted a child and adoption seemed like a good way for us to have a family and at the same time to fulfil a need in the community. We felt that we had good, relevant experience. We didn't want to foster as we wanted a child of our own, permanently.

Claire says: 'We were assessed as adopters and were on a waiting list for so long, it was clearly discrimination. Adoption services seem to have a vision of adopters being middle class, married heterosexuals but they can't always conceive of a different kind of family (single people, unmarried couples, same-sex couples). There was no reason not to approve us, so we were successful in being approved as potential adopters but nobody would actually place a child with us.'

We were advised to apply to become long-term foster carers as an alternative approach. This was absolutely the right advice. The fostering team embraced us straight away. They had no issue with us as a lesbian couple and placed Laila with us relatively quickly. We are now hoping the adoption will go ahead but it is frustrating that only one of us can legally adopt.

What advice would you give to people thinking about adoption?
On the basis of our experience, I would say don't bother to try for adoption in Northern Ireland until the law changes. In the meantime, I would approach it via long-term fostering.

You need to think about the emotional turmoil that the children have been through. For us, it was more like getting a three-year-old baby, who is much more demanding.

Be prepared for the intrusion of professionals. The children's social worker visits every 28 days. We also have meetings with our own link social worker, the child psychologist and other professionals, as well as medical appointments, LAC and other reviews, meetings with the school and childcare providers. It can add up to two or three meetings a week, every week. It would be hard for two people to hold down full-time jobs while fostering or adopting a child with complex needs.

Read about adoption and fostering and talk to people who have done it. Do your own research. Don't just rely on pretty pictures in the newspapers, advertising children. If children have been taken into care, there is a big reason for that. It means they have been living in severe circumstances and nobody else in their wider family could look after them.

For foster children, their future often hasn't been settled and it can be a very unstable time. People need to understand that. Sometimes children go back and forth between the birth and foster families before the matter of where the child will live permanently is settled.

What has been your experience of social workers?

They don't always seem to realise that people have different reasons for wanting to adopt or foster. Some people do it as a job but we are doing it to have a family.

Whenever a social worker visits us, Laila fears being taken away, she goes into a corner and rocks and has nightmares afterwards. She associates them with being taken into care and previous changes of placement.

Most of the paperwork doesn't account for single carers or same-sex couples but we managed to get the fostering team to change their materials. We found a lot of the fostering training was aimed at short-term fostering.

Social Services expect a lot from foster carers and don't always seem to understand what foster carers go through. We have come across some great social workers and some who are inconsistent or unclear.

What are some of the behavioural issues you have encountered?

Laila moved in when she was two-and-a-half. She hadn't learnt to speak and had a lot of nightmares and had obviously suffered trauma. For the first 15 months, she didn't sleep through the night. She could be violent and aggressive and break things. She would be very defiant and could go into a meltdown. We have found that any change is stressful for her, so we have to pre-empt it.

When she would lash out, you couldn't put her on the naughty step and leave her. You had to stay with her and try to calm her down. Most of the time, because of the attachment problems and early neglect or abuse, traditional parenting methods cannot be used or don't work. Things do get better as a child settles in with you. Laila used to wet the bed frequently but that has lessened now. She also sleeps better. When she is feeling sad, we give her a big hug and sometimes that brings things out into the open. We are generally very affectionate but Laila was desperate for affection, so we had to find a way to normalise it.

She now has settled periods, which can last several months but then other periods when she is extremely angry and anxious. We have to deal with her differently, depending on the circumstances. She responds very well to praise.

How was it when Laila first went to school?

We chose a school which had a good balance of social and educational support for children. We are very open with them. When Laila came to live with us, we wrote to the head teacher and went to see the school to talk about us fostering and hoping to adopt Laila.

When Laila first went to school, she would lash out. We went into the school and talked to the staff and they worked with her. Her aggression gradually decreased within six weeks. We take responsibility for her when she is at school, we don't think, oh, it's the teacher's problem.

Claire adds: 'Schools need to tune in to children with attachment disorder and realise that looked after children may have suffered trauma. Teachers definitely need more training and professional support.'

What do you think you have achieved?

I think if she hadn't come to live with us, Laila could have had ongoing problems because of her frustration and lack of communication skills. She may well have had to move schools several times. Laila's social and cognitive skills have developed so much. She is now doing well at school.

What impact has fostering had on your life?

It has had a huge impact – I changed jobs because my working environment wasn't supportive or flexible enough. I think long-term fostering should be given the same status as adoption in terms of leave and flexibility. Employers don't seem to recognise that it is a permanent arrangement.

It has also affected our social life. The amount of support a foster child needs makes it hard to leave Laila with a babysitter. We decided very early on that she wouldn't be able to cope with respite care either, so the only breaks we get are the ones we give each other.

We have had much less time for each other, we are physically more exhausted and our priority when we have time alone is to sort things out that we can't talk about in front of her. Our relationship was definitely on the back boiler for a while. Luckily, we communicate well and we can laugh about everyday stresses. We try to have some time together at the end of the day.

Claire adds: 'It has been like a bomb going off in the middle of our family but it has been a great experience. Laila is really good fun, full of life and wants a chance to move on and be happy. It has been brilliant but incredibly challenging. I wouldn't change it.'

How do you feel about not being a birth parent to Laila?

The blood tie is not important to me. I want my family to be part of Laila's identity. What's important for young children is the here and now. They want to know that they have uncles, grandparents, etc, with whom they can identify on a day-to-day basis. They will play more of a role in her everyday life than her birth family.

How much contact have you had with the birth parents?

We have met them both and developed a good relationship with them.

Have you talked to Laila about her past?

We have told her that her mother loved her but couldn't look after her. We don't know much about her father but we have told her what we know in an age-appropriate way. We don't pretend that she is not fostered or not waiting for adoption. We call her our forever girl, so she knows she is safe with us. We talk about how we looked for her and how lucky we were to find her.

We make scrap books and keep as much stuff as possible for souvenirs to go in her memory box.

We have actively sourced books and films with storylines that she can relate to, for example, Paddington Bear, Matilda or Stuart Little. she says: 'That's like me'. So many films have stories of abandoned children, she often relates to the characters.

What have you learned about yourself?

We work well as a family. I'm very proud of the way we have come together to support Laila and remain loyal to her. We have been very innovative. It has been a good experience for us, to knuckle down and get on with things. It has helped to form us as a family unit and we have become a lot stronger.

What, if any, difference do you think it has made being lesbian adopters or foster carers to your experience or your child's?

I don't think it is about your sexuality. I think it is about how good you are at supporting children. However, I think the LGBT community is a great, untapped resource for looked after children.

I think our experience of discrimination is useful in helping children who may also face discrimination on account of being in the care system.

I think being a same-sex couple has helped. We are very good at dividing responsibilities and supporting each other emotionally. We have always been good at communicating with each other.

Has your family been supportive?

My mother has welcomed Laila into the family and sees herself as her granny. Sometimes with family, it can be a bit tricky in terms of disclosing information. We have to tell them some things, such as the effect of neglect means that Laila says she's hungry all the time, even if she has just had breakfast.

How have other parents reacted?

Sometimes, I've had to stay at birthday parties due to Laila's feelings of insecurity. Sometimes other parents are curious. We don't explain our family set-up to everyone, only people we know well or will have an ongoing relationship with. Sometimes, we let people think whatever they like.

Have you been to any support groups?

We joined a local fostering network but we didn't feel that we fitted in as a gay couple. We went to the Christmas party but it just seemed to amplify our differences. Laila also thought it was a swap shop and that she would be given to another family. We keep in touch with the group and jump in and out of it as it suits us.

What impact has religion had on your fostering/adoption?

In Northern Ireland, there are two lists of people waiting to adopt – one each for Protestants and Catholics and you can't go on both. This is frustrating if you're not particularly religious or don't have a preference for which list you go on. They are not so fussy about fostering as the need to find homes is so much greater. The adoption team was more interested in religion; the fostering team have never asked about it.

What activities do you enjoy together?

Laila enjoys structured activities such as Brownies, swimming and other sports. We eat together most nights. We don't watch TV very much in the evenings but play games such as Monopoly. Laila goes to bed at 7.30.

What has been your experience of holidays?

We have to think very carefully about where we take Laila. She finds sleeping in a different bed scary and threatening, and can become very agitated and stressed by strange places.

To help to prepare her for this summer, we put together a scrap book of what we were going to do. We also have a timetable so she knows what to expect each day.

As a couple, we also need a holiday, so it can be stressful all round. Preparing her helps us all to enjoy it more.

What advice would you give about managing boundaries, sanctions, rewards, etc?

You need to stick to boundaries and make sure that sanctions and rewards mean something. You also need to put boundaries around activities, otherwise she would watch TV or play computer games for ever. One of the rewards we have is going to the playground in the early evening. Sanctions can involve removing toys or not letting her watch TV.

We never use food as treats or rewards. We use the step on the stairs as a sanction but we have to stay there with her. The maximum time is five minutes. We sometimes knock five minutes off bedtime but we never reduce the bedtime story, as this is part of her routine and keeps her feeling safe. You have to be careful with the use of sanctions not to remind children of their previous life.

Does Laila show you physical affection?

Claire says: 'She is very affectionate and spends a lot of time on my knee. She wants to be babied and sometimes grabs me around the neck, she is quite desperate for affection and can be a bit rough. It has taken some time to teach her not to be too rough. She likes it if you rub her back.'

She is not affectionate outside of the family. If anyone taps her on the shoulder, she'll flinch.

What is your opinion of safer caring policies?

I was wary about how much affection to show at the beginning.
Claire adds: 'We found it really difficult that we couldn't bring her into bed with us, as we were up three or four times a night. We would end up sitting on her floor by her bed, in the cold, hoping she would fall asleep.'

I understand that you need safeguarding policies but some of them seem a bit pointless. They wouldn't stop anyone abusing a child and they can make foster carers anxious about giving their foster children the affection they need.

Have you ever had any respite care?

No, Laila couldn't have coped with it. We have been really exhausted, as there have been nights when she hasn't slept at all, but she would have fallen apart if we had taken respite.

Are there any resources you would recommend?

Why Love Matters: How Affection Shapes a Baby's Brain by Sue Gerhardt (Routledge, 2004)

The Boy Who Was Raised As a Dog: And Other Stories from a Child Psychiatrist's Notebook – What Traumatized Children Can Teach Us About Loss, Love, and Healing by Dr Bruce Perry and Maia Szalavitz (Basic Books, 2008)

Attachment, Trauma and Resilience by Kate Cairns (BAAF, 2002)

Understanding Looked After Children: An Introduction to Psychology for Foster Care by Jeune Guishard-Pine, Suzanne McCall and Lloyd Hamilton (Jessica Kingsley Publishers, 2007)

What advice would you give to people who are fostering and adopting now?

It is OK to be angry and frustrated sometimes. Foster children, like any children, will push and pull you and prioritise themselves. You're only human, you need sleep and you are not infallible. Ultimately, you are doing a good job.

Give yourself breaks, take yourself off to a café, go to bed early or do whatever you need to do to restore yourself. If you are not functioning well, you will not be good for anyone.

Be prepared to stand up for your children and make sure they get the best chances. Don't be worried about putting people out. You need to sort out priorities. You have the whole picture and are living with the child day-in day-out. You are the expert, so don't be shy if you feel something is being omitted or underplayed!

Claire adds: 'Get all the support you can, be assertive and push for it. Sometimes you will have to battle the professionals but you need to be very determined and tough for the sake of your child.'

Afterword

Looking back over twenty-five years

Nora, now in her fifties, looks back on her experience of adoption for nearly twenty-five years and reflects on how attitudes towards lesbian and gay adoption have improved. Nora is now a single adoptive parent to an eleven-year-old girl and has two grandchildren by one of her two now adult adopted daughters. She and her daughter would like another adopted or fostered child to become part of their family.

In 1988, Nora, a part Irish and Jewish teacher and her partner, at the time, decided to apply to adopt. They found many local authorities and agencies were not even prepared to assess them as a lesbian couple. One inner London local authority did agree to assess them in 1989. They were approved over a year later. However, they then looked for over three years for a match with many homophobic responses and disappointments along the way.

In 1993, they took on a sibling placement of four girls, aged five, six, eight and nine. They all lived together for nearly two years but sadly the two older girls could not settle permanently. Nora and her partner went on to adopt the younger two, despite by that time having a very negative response from the authority which had originally placed them. When the youngest girl was 14, Nora adopted a baby girl, aged eleven months, who is now eleven years old.

Nora tells her story.

Why did you decide to adopt?

The first time, my then partner and I were very much together as a couple who wanted to have kids. At the same time, some more progressive local authorities were beginning to consider assessing lesbian couples, even though legally you couldn't adopt as a couple. However, they certainly weren't willing to assess gay male couples at that time. In our original assessment, the report said we were pioneers. I did not feel we were pioneers particularly, but that illustrates how infrequent it was at the time for out lesbians to adopt.

We were very clear that we were adopting together. It was very much a joint project, something we both wanted to do, and as two women in a partnership, it was obviously the most equal way that we could have kids. We also believed, as is still the case, that there are a lot of kids out there who need good homes and that we could provide one.

Even though we had a lot of difficulties with the four girls, and two of them eventually left us, I've never regretted our decision to adopt children and that is partly why I wanted to adopt again. I applied the second time around because I wanted the experience of bringing up a baby or a very young child. The youngest of the four girls was nearly six when they came to live with us and a lot has happened to children between birth and six, never mind in the womb.

So the second time around, I very much wanted a baby and I did toy with the idea of getting pregnant but it seemed crazy as it wasn't really what I wanted to do. However, I didn't seriously expect a local authority to consider me properly for a baby. Even by 2000, it was relatively rare for lesbians to be able to adopt babies. I suppose that is another indication of how much times have changed.

My second placement of a baby girl was in 2002. I was still with my partner at the time but we were very clear to Social Services that it was me who wanted to adopt again, with my partner supporting me.

Do you think attitudes have changed towards the assessment of lesbian and gay adopters and foster carers?

I would say my assessment process by two inner London boroughs in both cases was pretty fair, egalitarian and non-discriminatory. The difference was that the first time around we were really unusual and our social worker was also unusual in being willing to take on the assessment of a lesbian couple.

I was very impressed the second time around. We were incredibly lucky with the social worker who did the assessment. She was very aware. We were also able to be open about the fact that although we were still in a relationship, adopting again was something I particularly wanted to do.

When we were being assessed the second time, the local authority liked the fact that we had managed so well against really impossible odds with the older girls. They also liked that we had maintained contact with the two older siblings even though they were no longer living with us.

I'm still thinking of applying to foster long-term as they seem to have ruled me out for adoption, on age grounds, although they can't actually say that.

I think, once an authority has agreed to assess you, they are not usually overtly prejudiced during the assessment but when you are looking to get matched, there is still quite a lot of prejudice. Indeed, the social worker, who eventually placed my youngest daughter in 2002, said to the adoption team that she had never met anyone she knew was lesbian before, and was clearly making excuses as she was worried about it.

Do you think attitudes have changed towards the placement of children with lesbian and gay adopters and foster carers?

The first time, there was a big difference between the assessment and placement, with us actively looking for over three years for a match and encountering a great deal of homophobia along the way.

Initially, we had really bad luck, as the local authority which had assessed us had a sibling group that they were considering placing with us, because they thought that being placed with two women was the best possible solution for girls who had been abused. However, in the end, they couldn't place them with us as we had moved, unknowingly, to a street nearby to one of their grandmothers. After that, our approving local authority didn't have another suitable match, so we then got involved in a drawn-out, mostly discriminatory, search.

We knew we weren't being considered for matches just because we were lesbian. As an approved couple we hawked ourselves around, answering advertisements and ringing boroughs such as some in outer London, which I know now place children with gay male couples. I told them we'd been approved and asked if they could consider us. It was horrible hanging on the phone while they checked, especially when they came back and said, you would need to be married. I told them we couldn't be married even if we wanted to but they still said they would not consider us. It was absolutely awful. After a while we started writing to boroughs so at least the negative responses were at one remove, by letter.

Even the authority which eventually placed the four girls with us implied that it was very much touch and go whether they would take us to matching panel because they had never placed children with lesbians before.

There had been a pre-placement report and also the family finder recommended that our four girls be placed separately as their needs were so great that no one family could manage them. The placing authority originally came to see us about two different smaller sibling groups, and then right at the end of the interview asked if we would consider four. My "ex" didn't want four at first, but bit her lip and I was very positive about it and the rest is history. However, even once the decision was taken, the prejudice was horrendous. The Social Services department was buzzing with conversations about how this shouldn't be happening and our brave family finder, who looked so incredibly straight, came out as a lesbian, as a way of defending us. Her colleagues had all assumed she was straight.

There was terrible prejudice from the headteacher at their school. The girls never got to say a proper goodbye because he said it would be better for them to go back to where they came from than live with lesbians. We are not talking ancient history, we are talking 1993. I do think things are much better now. Yet, obviously we live in a society where even if new legislation reflects changes in societal attitudes, the kinds of attitudes and prejudice we experienced do not just completely go away.

The second time there was also a difference between the baby's social worker and the family finder team. The family finder link worker said she was embarrassed to ask but still asked if our home, which was quite big, would be heated enough for a baby. She was just looking for excuses because she was anxious about placing a baby with lesbians.

However, they liked the fact that I was good on multiculturalism. I'm Jewish and part Irish. This was important for finding the baby girl a family because she came from an ethnic mix which would have been hard to match.

I think the difference in attitudes between the adoption assessment social workers and the children's social workers is still very much there on the whole.

Do you think society's attitudes have changed towards lesbian and gay adoption and fostering?

When I first adopted, the appalling attitude of the girls' headteacher was still pretty prevalent. Most people in society still thought that if kids had to be adopted, the worst thing you could do was to place them with lesbians and gay men. Indeed, Stonewall did some research at the time, which sadly confirmed this attitude.

In terms of family, neighbours, schools and colleagues, once we had the four girls, I don't think people were that discriminatory. I think they were much more aware of the fact that we had taken on something really difficult that most other people would not have done. Also, they could see day to day that we were doing our best for our children.

Maybe that is why people are more positive now, because more people realise there are kids out there who need families and homes. Significantly, fewer people are prejudiced against lesbians and gay men more generally so they are less likely to be prejudiced against us adopting or fostering.

I don't think homophobia has been eradicated from our society, but we now live in a more open society, where people think about what is in the best interests of the child or children. This means that if there are lesbians and gay men willing to come forward as adoptive parents, most people think we should be considered equally.

I think probably the biggest change in attitude has been towards gay men adopting. When I was first adopting, I don't think gay men would have been considered at all. Some local authorities would consider lesbians because they thought two mothers were better than one and they were thinking that all children need a mother. I remember going to a meeting of lesbian adopters and potential lesbian and gay adopters in those days, and there were all these gay men there. I really felt for them. Gay men weren't getting a look in, whereas now a lot of gay men are getting children placed with them, as I think they should.

Obviously, a big legal change is the fact that lesbians and gay men can now adopt jointly as a couple and also be in a civil partnership.

I would say that some people still have a latent prejudiced attitude that if children have had a difficult start in life, then why give them another prejudice to deal with? I think some lesbians and gay men can also have this attitude themselves because they assume they won't have children and so have their own internalised oppression.

What impact do you think being a lesbian has had on your children's experiences?

I actually think it's a good thing for children being brought up by lesbians and also gay men. This is because by being a lesbian, no matter how much more accepted we are now in society, we are still different from what is conventionally the norm. At the end of the day, adopted kids are always going to be in a position of difference too. To be able to help an adopted child feel positive about their difference is a really good thing and something you can build on as a strength to offer them. I think adopted kids always do feel really different. As a result of their difficult early start in life, a lot seem to have difficulty making friends, or difficulty at school, even if they are adopted as babies.

My daughter doesn't seem to do badly but even she likes the support of other adopted kids, so there is something they have both been through that is similar. And now, they can have the support of other kids who have been adopted by lesbian or gay parents. I think it is really great that there are enough people around so the parents and the children can support each other. We have been camping three times with other lesbian and gay adopters and foster carers, and my daughter has really loved that.

And finally a word of advice to lesbian and gay adopters and foster carers...

I might start by saying be aware of what is going to happen with these children, even if they are baby placements. They are going to push a lot of buttons that you didn't even know you had. Don't just take your children's difficult behaviours at face value. Instead, try and sensitively support them to see what might have caused the behaviour. All children need boundaries but adopted children thrive with a creative and different response to their needs and boundary setting.

Be ready to instill a firm routine, negotiate and explain, praise good behaviour and gently nudge towards better behaviour. Encourage your children with activities like music or drama that they can shine at, rather than only what you want them to be good at, such as academic schoolwork.

Recognise that, as a lesbian or a gay man, you will have your own resilience to get you through and build on your own strength. Celebrate your difference. Enjoy the support of other parents and people who like children. Think about what makes you laugh and be ready to take pleasure in the world; that way, even when parenting is difficult, you might be able to defuse the situation with humour and laughter. Humour and laughter are very important ingredients to being an adoptive parent or foster carer. Enjoy that you will be challenged and grow. And if you really want to adopt or foster, I would say that having children come into your life is the best life-changing event you will ever experience.